itty-bitty toys

itty-bitty toys

susan b. anderson

photographs by liz banfield

ARTISAN
NEW YORK

ALSO BY SUSAN B. ANDERSON

Itty-Bitty Hats

Itty-Bitty Nursery

Published by Artisan
A Division of Workman Publishing Company, Inc.
225 Varick Street
New York, NY 10014-4381
www.artisanbooks.com

Library of Congress Cataloging-in-Publication Data
Anderson, Susan, B.
Itty-bitty toys / by Susan B. Anderson;
photographs by Liz Banfield
p. cm.
ISBN-13: 978-1-57965-376-7
1. Knitting—Patterns. 2. Soft toy making.
I. Title.
TT825.A555 2009
745.592'4—dc22   2009004059

Design by Jan Derevjanik

Printed in Malaysia
First printing, November 2009

1 3 5 7 9 10 8 6 4 2

This book is dedicated to the memory of my mother,

Mary Ann Barrett,

and to

my sweet, supportive family—

Brian, Evan, Ben, Holly & Mary Kate

contents

technique notebook

Knitting toys uses most of the same skills used in knitting a baby hat, a garment, or any other type of accessory. Sometimes the pieces are smaller and three-dimensional, which can make it feel like a new experience. Toy knitting uses the same skills in a different and interesting way. The following chapter provides instructions and tips on skills used throughout the book. If you are a new knitter, you'll need to get some basics down first, then move right on to your first project in chapter 2, referencing techniques as needed. I've included the methods that I use when knitting toys. However, there are no steadfast rules in knitting; do what feels right and comfortable for you. If you achieve the same result while going about the techniques in a different way, that is fine.

Now take a deep breath, jump right in, and have some fun!

the basics

There are certain skills that I think of when it comes to the basics of knitting. Knitters can easily access all of this information online or in books and be able to quickly gather and master the necessary skills. I extensively covered the basics of knitting in my last two books, *Itty-Bitty Hats* and *Itty-Bitty Nursery*, and on my blog through written and video tutorials at www.susanbanderson .blogspot.com and at SusanBAnderson on www.youtube.com. The following skills are covered in my previous books and on my blog: casting on, the knit stitch, the purl stitch, binding off, gauge, seaming, increases, and decreases.

A couple of longstanding and excellent teaching Web sites include:
    www.knittinghelp.com
    www.learntoknit.com

All the other techniques used for the projects in *Itty-Bitty Toys* are included on the following pages. Here's where you will find techniques that go beyond the basics. Every special technique you need to make the projects in this book is included on the following pages. If you are new to knitting, take your time and give it a go. You will have things figured out in no time.

KNITTING IN THE ROUND

knitting in the round on circular needles • Circular needles are two needles that are joined by a cable. They are used for both knitting in the round and knitting back and forth. The length of the needles, measured from tip to tip, is determined by the cable length. Even though the needles are attached, consider them separate needles, holding one needle in your right hand and the other in your left hand. The following steps will start you on your way.

1. Cast on just as you would if you were knitting back and forth.

2. After you have completed casting on, spread the stitches all the way around the needles and the cable so the first and last stitches come together at the points of the needles.

3. *Most important,* make sure the stitches are not twisted before you begin knitting. Look to see if the cast-on row is at the inside of the circle as you hold the needles up. If the stitches are twisted, then untwist them at this time. There is no way to untwist stitches once you've started knitting. The only way to fix this is to start over.

4. Place a stitch marker (see page 16) on the right needle before you begin knitting, to mark the beginning of the round. Do this by sliding a stitch marker onto the point of your right needle.

5. Hold the left needle in your left hand and the right needle in your right hand. Be sure the yarn is coming from the needle in your right hand.

6. Begin working in the round by knitting the first stitch on the left needle as you usually would (again, making sure the yarn is coming from your right needle). Now you have joined the circle.

7. Continue knitting as your pattern directs until you reach your desired length, slipping the stitch marker from the left to the right needle as you begin each new round. Slide the stitches along the cable as you knit.

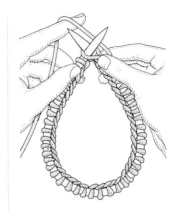

• The easy part of knitting in the round is that you are knitting in a continuous circle, there is no turning back and forth, and there are no seams to sew at the end. Many people prefer knitting in the round over any other kind of knitting due to this continuity.

knitting in the round on double-pointed needles • When you are knitting in the round on a number of stitches too small to fit comfortably around a circular needle, you must use double-pointed needles. Double-pointed needles come in different lengths. Certain lengths of needles are better suited for certain projects. You'll have to experiment to find a length that feels good to you.

Some projects call for double-pointed needles right away, on the cast-on row, and other projects transfer onto double-pointed needles as the stitches decrease in number. I will describe both types of situations. For this book, most often you will use four double-pointed needles, with the stitches being divided on three needles and the fourth needle being used to knit onto. Sometimes a pattern calls for five double-pointed needles to be used.

transferring stitches from circular needles to double-pointed needles • Following are the steps for transferring from a circular needle to double-pointed needles when it becomes too tight.

1. With the left circular needle in your left hand, begin knitting onto the first double-pointed needle. Knit as many stitches onto the first needle as directed in the pattern. Switch to the second double-pointed needle, which is empty, and begin knitting the required number of stitches onto this needle, being sure to pull the yarn snugly when transferring to this new needle. Do the same for the third needle. The three double-pointed needles form a triangle with the first and last stitches meeting at the beginning of the round.

TIP • Some patterns will tell you how many stitches to put on each needle. Others will tell you to divide the stitches evenly onto three or four needles.

2. Be sure to keep track of the beginning of your round by placing a detachable stitch marker on the first stitch.

3. Begin knitting in the round just as you would with circular needles. Hold the first needle in your left hand, ready to knit. Hold the empty fourth needle in your right hand. This fourth needle is your working needle. Concentrate only on the needle you are knitting from and the working needle, basically ignoring the other needles. Insert the right needle into the first stitch on the left needle and knit as usual. Knit all the stitches on the first needle. When this needle is empty, it becomes your working needle.

4. Hold the second needle in your left hand with the stitches ready to knit. Begin knitting the stitches onto the empty needle in your right hand. Knit all of the stitches on the second needle onto the working needle in your right hand. Make sure you pull the yarn snugly when starting a new needle so you don't create gaps along the way.

5. Knit across the stitches on the third and final needle to complete one round.

* Continue knitting in the round this way and decrease stitches as the pattern directs.

knitting in the round on double-pointed needles from the cast-on row •
This type of knitting with double-pointed needles is used often, especially when knitting smaller tubes or spherical shapes.

1. Cast on all required stitches onto one double-pointed needle.

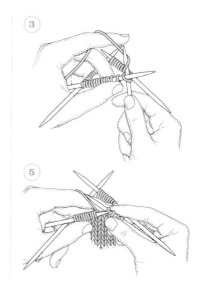

2. Knit the first round onto the double-pointed needles, dividing the stitches evenly onto three needles.

3. Hold the three needles so they form a triangle, with the first and last stitches meeting at the beginning of the round and the working yarn coming from the right needle.

4. *Most important*, check to make sure the cast-on stitches are not twisted around any of the needles before you begin knitting.

5. With the empty fourth needle held in your right hand, insert the point into the first stitch on the first needle, which is held in your left hand. Focus only on the two working needles, ignoring the other needles. Knit as usual until all stitches are knit from the first needle. Now empty, it becomes your working needle.

6. Work the same way across the other two needles, being sure to pull the yarn snugly when transferring from one needle to the next.

7. After completing one round, place a stitch marker to show the beginning of the round on the first stitch.

• Continue knitting in the round as your pattern directs.

casting a small number of stitches onto double-pointed needles • There are a couple of different ways to do this. The first is to cast all of the stitches onto one double-pointed needle and then transfer the stitches onto the appropriate needles. The other is to cast the stitches onto the three double-pointed needles from the start. Let's say, for example, you are going to cast 9 stitches onto three double-pointed needles. You can cast on 3 stitches on each of 3 double-pointed needles. As you are casting on, make sure to pull the yarn so it is snug between the needles.

Next you will start the first round. Join to work in the round by starting to knit on the first stitch of the first needle. Place a stitch marker on the first stitch of the first needle, and make sure that the row of cast-on stitches is not spiraled around the needle. There should be no twists in the row. When you are starting to knit with a small number of stitches, the needles can feel kind of floppy and awkward. Don't worry about this; just start working, and before you start each needle for the first round, double check that the stitches on it aren't twisted around the needle. Once you work a few rounds, it becomes much easier. In toy patterns, you will often increase your stitches over the first several rounds.

INCREASING

Increases are used when you want to make your knitted piece wider. You do this by adding stitches as you go.

knit into the front and back of the same stitch, or kfb

1. Knit the first stich and leave it on the left needle.

2. Insert the tip of the right needle into the back of the same stitch and knit again.

3. Slip the stitch off the left needle. Two stitches have been made from 1 stitch and are now on the right needle.

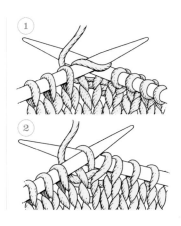

purl into the front and back of the same stitch, or pfb

1. Purl the first stitch and leave it on the left needle.

2. Insert the tip of the right needle through the back of the same stitch from left to right and bring the point to the front. Purl again.

3. Slip the stitch off the left needle. Two stitches have been made from 1 stitch and are now on the right needle.

make one, or m1 • Look at the bar between the stitches on the needles.

1. Insert the left needle under the top bar from front to back, bringing the bar onto the left needle.

2. Knit the bar on the left needle through the back loop.

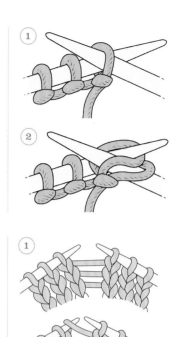

DECREASING

Decreases are used when you want to make your piece narrower at a certain point, as at the end of a duck's beak. You do this by making fewer stitches as you go.

knit 2 stitches together, or k2tog • This makes a right-slanting decrease.

1. With the right needle, and the yarn in back, put the point through the first 2 stitches on the left needle at the same time as if to knit.

2. Knit these 2 stitches together to make 1 stitch on the right needle.

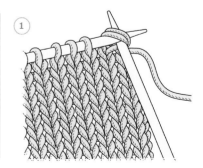

purl 2 stitches together, or p2tog • This makes a right-slanting decrease.

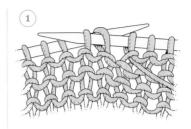

1. With the right needle, and the yarn in front, put the point through the first 2 stitches on the left needle at the same time as if to purl.

2. Purl these 2 stitches together to make 1 stitch on the right needle.

slip stitch, slip stitch, knit 2 stitches together through the back loops, or ssk (slip, slip, knit) • This makes a left-slanting decrease.

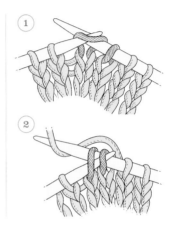

1. With the right needle and the yarn in back of the work, slip the first 2 stitches onto the right needle as if to knit.

2. With the left needle, put the point through the front of the 2 slipped stitches on the right needle.

3. Knit the 2 slipped stitches together by wrapping the yarn around the right needle and pulling a loop through onto the right needle, making 1 stitch on the right needle.

i-cord • I-cord is a tried and true embellishment that has endless uses. For this collection, it is used for loops, arms and legs, and much more. The versatility of this knitted cord makes it a must for every knitter to learn. Here are the steps for making I-cord:

1. Using a double-pointed needle, cast on 2, 3, or 4 stitches, depending on how thick you want your cord. Knit these stitches using another double-pointed needle and do not turn the work.

2. Slide the stitches to the other end of the double-pointed needle. The yarn will now be on the opposite side of the work.

3. Bring the yarn very firmly around the back of the work and knit the stitches firmly to create a tube. Do not turn.

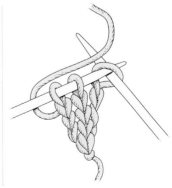

• Repeat rows 2 and 3 until the cord reaches the desired length. Bind off. Cut the yarn and pull it through the last stitch.

   TIP • When knitting I-cord, gently pull down on the cord as it forms. This helps the stitches to fall in place to better form the cord.

sewing on an appliqué • Sewing on appliqués is not difficult and allows for some extra creativity. Knitted fabric is so pliable that you can create different shapes by stretching and molding the appliqué as you sew. When knitting the appliqués in this book, remember to leave a longer tail that can later be used for sewing the appliqué onto the toy.

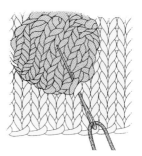

1. Arrange the appliqués and pin them to the toy. Thread a tail end or piece of matching yarn on a yarn needle.

2. Work around the outer edge of the appliqué, turning your work as you go. Pick up a stitch on the toy, sew through the outermost edge of the appliqué, and pull the yarn through. Repeat all the way around the appliqué.

3. Pull the end through to the inside.

pick up stitches • To pick up and knit stitches is a skill that every knitter needs to master. It is used in knitting toys and is an easy way to continue knitting onto another piece of knitted fabric.

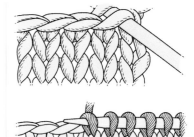

Pick up stitches means that you will be picking up stitches along an edge or another place on the fabric as if you are going to knit them. You will insert the needle into your knitted fabric, wrap the yarn as if you were knitting, and draw a stitch through the knitted fabric. Put each new stitch on your right needle. Be careful not to create holes as you work by making sure you insert the needle into the correct point on the knitted piece. The pattern will tell you how many stitches to pick up.

Pick up and knit from a bound-off edge.

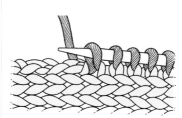

1. With the yarn held to the back of your piece and the right side of your work facing you, take one needle in your right hand and insert the needle from front to back (right through the fabric), into each stitch just beneath the cast-on edge, bind-off edge, or one stitch in on a side edge.

2. Wrap the yarn as if to knit and pull the loop through the fabric, leaving the new stitch on the right needle.

Pick up and knit from a side edge.

kitchener stitch • Kitchener stitch is used to graft live stitches together. This means that the two sets of stitches are joined in a way that is continuous, without any seam.

1. Place the stitches to be grafted so they are evenly divided on two needles with the points of the needles facing to the right, and the needles parallel so one needle is in front and the other is in back. The wrong sides of the fabric are facing each other.

2. With a length of matching yarn threaded into a yarn needle, insert the yarn needle through the first stitch on the front needle as if to knit, and drop it off of the needle.

3. Insert the yarn needle through the second stitch on the front needle as if to purl. Do not drop that stitch off of the needle; pull the yarn through.

4. On the back needle, insert the yarn needle through the first stitch as if to purl and drop it off of the needle.

5. Insert the needle through the second stitch on the back needle as if to knit. Do not drop that stitch off of the needle; pull the yarn through.

• Repeat steps 2 through 5 until the stitches are all off of the needles. Weave in the end on the wrong side.

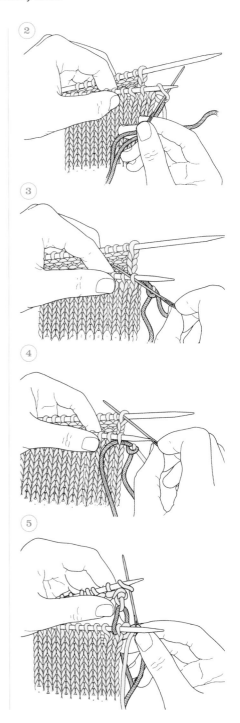

FINISHING OR SEAMING

Sewing garter stitch edges together is simple and, best of all—due to the bumpy nature of the fabric—it is forgiving. This basic seaming technique is perfect for sewing together squares for the Nesting Boxes or the sides of the Penguin.

garter stitch seam • With the edges you wish to join lined up next to each other and right sides facing you, cut a length of yarn and thread it on a yarn needle so you are working with a single thickness of yarn. Do not knot the end of the yarn. Starting at the left edge, insert the needle into the top loop (a purl stitch bump) and draw the yarn through the loop nearly to the end. Leave a 3-inch tail. On the corresponding stitch on the right edge, insert the needle into the bottom loop (a knit stitch). Do not draw the stitches up too tightly—try to match the tightness of the knitting, but do not leave gaps in the seam. Continue alternating the sides with a top loop and a bottom loop. When the seam is completed, weave in both ends of the seaming yarn and trim close to the knitted piece.

GARTER STITCH SEAM
Insert the yarn needle into the top bump on one side, then the bottom loop of the corresponding stitch on the other side. Continue to alternate in this way.

whipstitch seam • With the edges you wish to join lined up next to each other and right sides facing you, cut a length of yarn and thread it on a yarn needle. Starting on the right side, insert the needle into the stitch at the edge. On the corresponding stitch on the left edge, insert the needle. Gently pull the yarn through, keeping an even tension. The whipstitch seam can be used on any type of knitted piece.

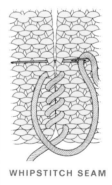

WHIPSTITCH SEAM

mattress stitch • This is a great technique for making an invisible seam.

1. Lay the pieces flat with the right sides facing up. Pin the pieces together with safety pins if necessary. Thread a tail end or new piece of yarn through a yarn needle, and begin sewing at the bottom of the seam.

2. Working upward, find the bars, or horizontal strands, between the first stitch and second stitch up the sides of the pieces. You can do this by gently pulling apart the two stitches.

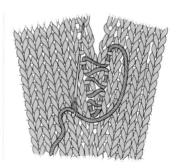

3. Put the needle under the first two bars on one side and draw the yarn through. Then place it under the two bars directly opposite on the other piece and draw the yarn through. Repeat back and forth this way, working up the seam two bars at a time on each side. As you go, be sure to insert the needle into the last "hole" you came out of on each side.

• Complete by weaving in the end along the seam on the inside of the piece and trim.

NOTE • You can whipstitch two edges or two parts of a toy together. It can be used as a decorative stitch on the right side of the fabric, or it can be used as an invisible seam on the wrong side of the fabric. Basically, you are wrapping the yarn around the outer edge or across two surfaces of the fabric.

CROCHET TECHNIQUES

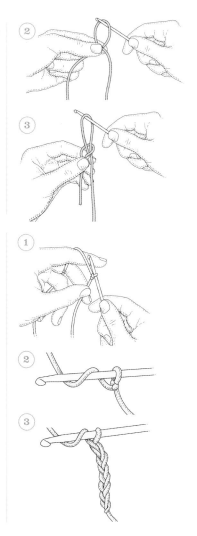

slipknot • The slipknot is the very first step to begin crochet.

1. Measure out about 4 inches from the tail end of the ball of yarn. You will make a slip knot at this point on the yarn.

2. Make a loop, overlapping the yarn at the bottom of the loop.

3. Bring the yarn that is on top of the overlap behind and then through the loop, making another loop. Pull up.

4. Put the new loop on the hook and tighten it to fit.

chain sitch • The chain stitch is the place to start when learning to crochet. With a slipknot on the hook, and the hook in your right hand, and with your left hand holding the working yarn as you would for continental knitting (reversed if you're left-handed), continue as follows:

1. Wrap the yarn over the hook from back to front (counterclockwise).

2. Catching the yarn with your hook, pull it through the loop on the hook. (You may need to hold the slipknot with the thumb and middle finger of your left hand to keep it steady.)

3. Repeat steps 1 and 2 until desired number of chain stitches are made.

slip stitch • The slip stitch is often used to join rounds when crocheting in a circle or when making a picot edging.

1. Insert the hook into the two upper strands of the appropriate stitch as directed in the pattern.

2. Wrap the yarn over the hook from back to front (counterclockwise) and pull it through the stitch.

3. With two loops on the hook, pull the second loop through the first loop.

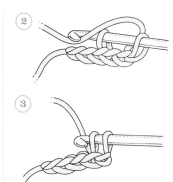

single crochet • The single crochet is one of the first stitches you'll need to learn. It is the most basic stitch, but it can be used to create almost anything.

1. Insert the hook into the two upper strands of the appropriate stitch as directed in the pattern.

2. Wrap the yarn over the hook from back to front (counterclockwise) and pull it through the stitch.

3. Wrap the yarn over the hook once more and pull it through both loops.

• Repeat as directed.

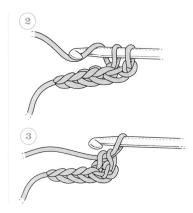

double crochet • Double crochet makes a higher stitch than single crochet.

1. Wrap the yarn over the hook and insert the hook under the two upper strands of the stitch.

2. Wrap the yarn over the hook and pull it through. (3 loops on hook)

3. Wrap the yarn over the hook and pull it through. (2 loops on hook)

4. Wrap the yarn over the hook and pull it through the remaining 2 loops (1 loop on hook)

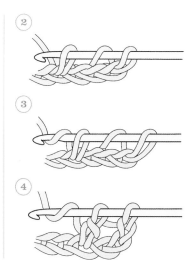

EMBROIDERY TECHNIQUES

spiderweb • This embroidery technique is one of my favorites for making dots on knitted fabric. It is simple, quick, and fun.

1. Begin by making 5 straight stitches radiating out from a center point. These stitches form spokes and are the foundation for the spiderweb.

2. Next, stitching up from the center, begin weaving the needle over and under the spokes until they are completely covered.

3. Pull the yarn through to the wrong side of the fabric and secure by taking a few small stitches. Trim the end close to the fabric.

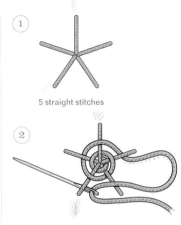

5 straight stitches

Stitch over and under the spokes until the straight stitches are covered

backstitch • The backstitch is used to make lines that are straight or curved. Make the stitches small and as even as possible.

1. Cut a length of yarn and thread it on a yarn needle. Pull the yarn through several loops on the wrong side of the fabric, leaving a ½-inch tail. With the needle, pull the yarn through to the right side at your starting point (1).

2. Moving backward from your starting point, insert your needle at 2 and have the point of the needle come out at 3. This should be one motion.

3. Pull the yarn through. This is your new starting point (1). Insert the needle into the new 2, and have the point of the needle come out at the new 3.

• Keep working in this way, moving backward and forward, until you have completed the length of stitching desired. At the last stitch, pull the yarn through to the back and weave in the end on the wrong side of the knitted fabric.

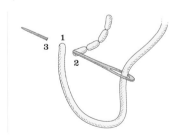

satin stitch • The satin stitch is used to fill in spaces and to create shapes. It is worked in one motion and moves quickly.

1. Cut a length of yarn and thread it on a yarn needle. Pull the yarn through several loops on the wrong side of the fabric. Pull the needle through to the right side, at the starting point (1).

2. Insert the needle at 2 and have the point of the needle come out at 3. Pull the yarn through. This is your new starting point (1).

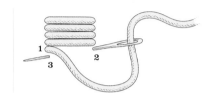

• Repeat step 2 until the space is filled. On the last stitch, pull the yarn through to the wrong side of the knitted fabric and weave in the end.

running stitch

1. Cut a length of yarn and thread it on a yarn needle. Pull the yarn through several loops on the wrong side of the fabric. Pull the yarn through to the right side. This is your starting point (1).

2. Insert the needle at 2 and bring it up at 3, pulling the yarn through in one motion.

3. Insert the needle at 4 and bring it up at 5, pulling the yarn through in one motion.

• Repeat to the end for the desired length. Pull the yarn through to the wrong side of the knitted fabric. Weave in the end.

straight stitch

1. Cut a length of yarn and thread it on a yarn needle. Pull the yarn through several loops on the wrong side of the fabric. Pull the needle through to the open middle of the knitted hole. This is the starting point (1).

2. Insert the needle at 2 and bring the needle back through the open middle. Pull the yarn through.

3. Insert the needle at 3 and bring the needle back through the open middle. Pull the yarn through.

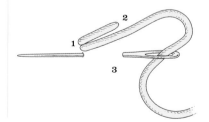

• Continue in this way until you have filled in around the border of the hole. You may have to overlap the stitches somewhat to get a solid look. Don't worry if all of the stitches are not the exact same length; this adds more character. Mine aren't and probably never will be.

wrapping stitch • This is my variation on both the overcast stitch and a couching embroidery technique, but it is slightly different because it isn't exactly like either of these stitches of old. I use this technique a lot for the eyes of the toys.

1. Using a straight stitch as the foundation for the shape or line you intend to wrap, thread a 12- to 18-inch piece of yarn on a yarn needle. Secure the yarn on the wrong side of the fabric by taking a couple of small stitches through the straight stitches. Bring the needle and the yarn to the right side of the fabric, at the starting point.

2. Next make tiny satin stitches around the straight stitches. The pattern will tell you how many wraps to make.

3. After the last stitch is completed, pull the yarn through to the inside of the toy, and cut the end close to the fabric.

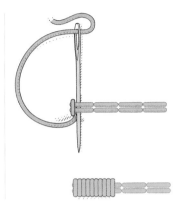

french knots • I use French knots a couple of times in this book (for the Zebra puppet and the Santa doll). It's a great decorative stitch. However, my French knots, even when done exactly according to others' instructions, never turn out quite right. So here is my own twist on this technique.

1. Cut a length of yarn and thread it on a yarn needle. Pull the yarn through several loops on the wrong side of the fabric. Pull the yarn through to the right side of the fabric. This will place the French knot.

2. Wrap the yarn around the needle three times while holding the needle close to the fabric. Hold the yarn wraps taut by pinching the yarn between your left thumb and index finger. Insert the needle nearby and pull it gently through to the wrong side of the fabric.

3. Insert the needle right next to the wraps and pull the yarn through to the right side of the fabric.

4. Insert the needle into the center of the knot just created and pull it through to the wrong side of the fabric. This extra stitch makes the French knot much more secure and gives it a finished look.

• If you are making one knot, cut the yarn and weave in the end. If you are making many knots, carry the yarn over the back of your work to different spots, but only if you can't see the carried yarn through the fabric. If you can see it from the right side, you'll have to cut your yarn and tie it off for each French knot, then reattach the yarn at the new spots as you go.

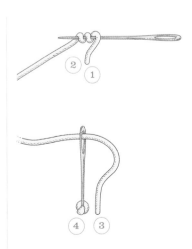

TOY-KNITTING TIPS

KNITTING IN THE ROUND is the best way to construct most knitted toys. I have made many toys that are knit in flat pieces that then needed to be seamed up the sides and sewn together at the end. That's a lot of sewing, which gets tedious. When you create the parts of the toy in their actual round shape, it eliminates nearly all of the seaming; then you only need stitch the parts together to finish your fabulous toy. Easy!

STITCH TOGETHER AS YOU GO is my mantra while making toys. Remember in home economics when your teacher told you to put away your ingredients as you go so you won't have so much clean up at the end? That's exactly my philosophy when you are making the parts of a toy. By sewing the parts together as you finish them, you won't be overwhelmed at the end by having to sew the entire toy together. What makes this even better is that you can see your toy come to life bit by bit as you work, and that can be very motivating. When you knit your last part and attach it, your toy will be pretty much finished.

DOUBLE-POINTED NEEDLES are not to be feared. I think they often don't get a fair shake with some knitters. Using double-pointed needles is not any more difficult than knitting in the round with circulars. They are wonderful tools for taking control of your knitting. You can easily manipulate the shape and form of a knitted item when using them, so they are my favorite needles for toy knitting and for creating other small knitted objects. I strongly suggest that you take the time to feel comfortable with them. The more you practice, the easier it will become.

STITCH MARKERS are important for marking the beginning of a round and for keeping track of specific rounds in the pattern. I suggest that you use the detachable plastic stitch markers that look similar to an oversize safety pin. That way, you can remove and place markers without having them locked in anywhere on your knitting or on your needles.

STITCH TO SECURE AND WEAVING IN ENDS on a closed toy that is worked in the round is different because you can't get to the wrong side of the fabric. After threading the tail on a yarn needle, pull the tail through the remaining stitches and gather them tight to close the hole. Run the needle through the remaining stitches a couple more times. Pull the end to the inside and then poke the needle back through the right side of the fabric to draw the end to the outside again. Pull the end slightly taut and trim close to the knitted fabric. The end should then pop back inside of the toy and stay this way. I do this for all of the toy parts and for the embroidery on the faces.

FACES are sometimes the most difficult and always the most important part of a toy. Usually I don't have to try things more than once with my knitting, but when embroidering the faces, sometimes I do. It can be difficult to get the eyes even or the nose in the center, or to achieve a certain expression. If your stitches don't look correct the first time, pull them right back out and keep trying until you are satisfied.

POLY PELLETS are little plastic beads that are found in craft stores in the doll-making aisle. These are fantastic for partially filling your knitted toys, because they give a nice heft or substance to them. However, if your fabric is not tightly knit, the pellets may push through and actually pop out. Most of my toys are tightly knit on smaller than usual needles so the pellets won't fall through; however, it does still raise a concern if you are knitting for babies and young children. The pellets are considered a **choking hazard** for babies and toddlers and even young children. If you are concerned about creating a **choking hazard, *do not use*** the poly pellets for filling or stuffing your toys. Only use the polyester fiberfill. Your toy will be lighter in weight, but you won't have to worry about anyone choking. A **muslin bag** can be used to hold the poly pellets and remedy the choking hazard for babies and young children. You could sew up or purchase a simple muslin or other cotton fabric bag (drawstring sachet bags work perfectly) to fill with poly pellets and then place it inside the base of your toy. Then stuff the rest of the toy with polyester fiberfill. This way the pellets are contained and can't sneak out through the knitted fabric.

SMALLER NEEDLES than what is suggested on the corresponding yarn labels are used for knitting the projects in this collection. There are a few reasons for this. First, when knitting toys you want to achieve a dense, tight fabric so the toy has form and shape. If you knit too loosely, even at the suggested gauge for a yarn, your toy will become a shapeless lump before long. The second reason is that you don't ever want to see the stuffing showing through the surface of your toy; that's a major no-no. The last reason is that a dense fabric subjected to wear and tear will stand the test of time much better.

THE AMOUNT OF POLYESTER FIBERFILL to purchase will vary depending on your plans. If you are going to make one, two, or even three of the smaller-size toys, one small bag of fiberfill will be plenty. If you are planning on making many or all of the toys in the book, one large bag will most likely be enough. I always grab a couple of large bags to keep at home so I never run out.

A NOTE ABOUT ORGANIC YARNS

LIVING AN ORGANIC LIFESTYLE has become increasingly popular recently, and the knitting community has responded accordingly by making more and more organic yarns available. When knitting for children and babies, we need to be especially concerned with the fiber content of the yarns we select and the environmental impact the materials we use may have. That is why so many of the projects in this book are made using organic yarns: all of the reversible projects, the Baby Doll Set, Mama Duck and Ducklings, the Lamb, the Matryoshka dolls, the Penguin, the Pig, the Bunny, the Wrap-Me-Up Puppies, the Squishies, and the Koala Mama and Baby. Some of the yarns are dyed, and some represent the gorgeous variety of natural shades of wool and cotton, but all were chosen to make their project absolutely shine.

(2)

quick and easy

There is nothing better than a simple project that also looks great. Beginners appreciate easy projects, of course, but all levels of knitters love projects that can be completed with ease and style.

The four projects in this chapter take you through the skills necessary to complete those in the rest of the book.

As you start with a couple of garter-stitch-square projects and move into creating a simple ball shape on double-pointed needles, you'll build confidence and pick up some new skills. Jump right in and don't be intimidated by new techniques—embrace them!

nesting boxes

I learned everything about babies from my mom, who always knew exactly how to make a baby laugh. With all of the grandkids, she would stack plastic nesting boxes or cups and then let the child knock them down. Babies get so much fun out of this, and of course they'll do it over and over again.

When a baby knocks the stack of my knitted nesting boxes down, it won't be quite so loud. I used plastic mesh and fabric to finish off the inside of this simple project and to make the boxes sturdier. Garter stitch looks great from both sides, so you can leave them unlined if you choose. An added bonus is that the boxes are beautiful and can be used for storage in your knitting studio or around the house, not just for baby entertainment.

finished measurements
- Large Box: 5 x 5 x 5 inches
- Medium Box: 3¾ x 3¾ x 3¾ inches
- Small Box: 2½ x 2½ x 2½ inches
- Extra-Small Box: 1¼ x 1¼ x 1¼ inches

yarn
- Rowan Handknit Cotton (100% cotton; 93 yards/50 grams), 1 skein each in Thunder #335, Ice Water #239, Turkish Plum #277, Tangerine Dream #337, Gooseberry #219, Rose #332, Double Chocolate #315, Bermuda #324, and Tope #253

tools
- U.S. size 4 needles, 24-inch circular or straight needles, or size needed to obtain gauge
- Tape measure or ruler
- Yarn needle
- Scissors
- Cotton fabric to line the inside of the boxes (optional), small amounts to cover finished measurements (see above) plus ¼ inch on all sides
- Sewing needle and matching thread (optional)
- 3 sheets of 12 x 18 inch plastic mesh (optional)

gauge
- 5½ stitches per inch in garter stitch

large box
sides 1 and 2
With Thunder, cast on 27 stitches. Work in garter stitch (knit every row) throughout.

stripe pattern
Rows 1–4: Thunder
Rows 5–8: Ice Water
   Repeat rows 1–8 until the side measures 5 inches from the cast-on edge, ending with either row 4 or row 8. Bind off. Cut the yarn, leaving an 8-inch-long tail, and pull through the remaining stitch.

sides 3 and 4
With Thunder, cast on 27 stitches.

stripe pattern
Rows 1–4: Thunder
Rows 5–8: Turkish Plum
   Complete as for sides 1 and 2.

bottom
With Thunder, cast on 27 stitches and begin working in garter stitch. Continue until the bottom measures 5 inches from the cast-on edge. Bind off. Cut the yarn, leaving an 8-inch-long tail, and pull through the remaining stitch.

finishing option 1
Holding together the side edges of two pieces having alternating stripe patterns, thread one

bound-off tail on a yarn needle and whipstitch together. Whipstitch the remaining two unattached side pieces to either side of the two joined pieces, then whipstitch the unattached edges together to form a box. Whipstitch the bottom to one end of the box, using a bound-off tail. Weave all ends to the inside and trim.

finishing option 2

For each side piece and the bottom, cut a piece of the plastic mesh, trimming the mesh ¼ inch smaller on all sides than the knitted piece. With the thread and sewing needle, tack down each corner of the plastic mesh to the knitted piece with a few stitches.

Attach the four side pieces as in Finishing Option 1, but do not yet join the final edges to form a box. Lay the attached side pieces flat on a table on top of the lining fabric. Pin the knitted piece to the fabric and cut out the lining, leaving a ¼-inch seam allowance on all sides.

Fold ¼ inch of the fabric toward the wrong side on all edges, to match the size of the knitted piece. Pin the folded fabric to the knitted piece, wrong side of the fabric facing the plastic mesh. With the sewing needle and matching thread, whipstitch the fabric to the knitted sides.

Repeat for the bottom piece.

Join the final unattached sides of the piece to form a box.

Whipstitch the bottom piece to the sides with a bound-off tail threaded on a yarn needle.

medium box

sides 1 and 2

With Tangerine Dream, cast on 21 stitches. Work in garter stitch (knit every row) throughout.

stripe pattern

Rows 1–4: Tangerine Dream
Rows 5–8: Gooseberry

Repeat rows 1–8 until the side measures 3¾ inches from the cast-on edge, ending with either row 4 or row 8. Bind off. Cut the yarn, leaving an 8-inch tail, and pull through the remaining stitch.

sides 3 and 4

With Gooseberry, cast on 21 stitches.

stripe pattern

Rows 1–4: Gooseberry
Rows 5–8: Tangerine Dream

Complete as for sides 1 and 2.

bottom

With Gooseberry, cast on 21 stitches and begin working in garter stitch. Continue until the bottom measures 3¾ inches from the cast-on edge. Bind off. Cut the yarn, leaving an 8-inch-long tail, and pull through the remaining stitch.

Finish using Option 1 or Option 2 as for the Large Box.

small box

sides 1 and 2

With Rose, cast on 15 stitches. Work in garter stitch (knit every row) throughout.

stripe pattern

Rows 1–4: Rose
Rows 5–8: Double Chocolate

Repeat rows 1–8 until the side measures 2½ inches from the cast-on edge, ending with either row 4 or row 8. Bind off. Cut the yarn, leaving a 6-inch tail, and pull through the remaining stitch.

sides 3 and 4

With Double Chocolate, cast on 15 stitches.

stripe pattern

Rows 1–4: Double Chocolate
Rows 5–8: Rose

Complete as for sides 1 and 2.

bottom

With Rose, cast on 15 stitches and begin working in garter stitch. Continue until the bottom measures 2½ inches from the cast-on edge. Bind off. Cut the yarn, leaving a 6-inch-long tail, and pull through the remaining stitch.

Finish using either Option 1 or Option 2 as for the Large Box.

extra-small box

sides 1 and 2

With Bermuda, cast on 9 stitches. Work in garter stitch (knit every row) throughout.

color pattern

Rows 1 and 2: Bermuda

Switch to Tope and continue in garter stitch until the side measures 1¼ inches from the cast-on edge. Bind off. Cut the yarn, leaving a 6-inch tail, and pull through the remaining stitch.

sides 3 and 4

With Tope, cast on 9 stitches. Work in garter stitch (knit every row) throughout.

color pattern

Rows 1 and 2: Tope

Switch to Bermuda and continue in garter stitch until the side measures 1¼ inches from the cast-on edge. Bind off. Cut the yarn, leaving a 6-inch tail, and pull through the remaining stitch.

bottom

With Tope, cast on 9 stitches and begin working in garter stitch. Continue until the bottom measures 1¼ inches from the cast-on edge. Bind off. Cut the yarn, leaving a 6-inch-long tail, and pull through the remaining stitch.

Finish using either Option 1 or Option 2 as for the Large Box.

squishies

Nothing is better than a squishy knitted ball. Throw them, roll them, chew them (babies only, please), display them in a big bowl . . . the sky is the limit.

Squishies are also the perfect skill-building project. Without a doubt, double-pointed needles are my favorite tools, and getting familiar with them will open every door in the knitting world. This small, quick-to-finish project packs in important techniques that are used throughout *Itty-Bitty Toys*.

Be patient, take your time, and you'll reap the benefits as soon as you finish your first one. I promise you'll want to make a dozen more right away.

finished measurements
- Large: 4 inches tall
- Medium: 3 inches tall
- Small: 2 inches tall

yarn
- Blue Sky Dyed Cotton (100% cotton: 150 yards/100 grams); 1 skein makes many Squishies
- Large: Poppy #601, Flamingo #627, Lemongrass #607, and Pickle #633
- Medium: Lemongrass #607 and Caribbean #630
- Small: Orchid #618, Ladybug #629, Flamingo #627, and Pickle #633

tools
- U.S. size 6 set of four double-pointed needles, or size needed to obtain gauge
- Stitch marker
- Yarn needle
- Scissors
- Polyester fiberfill, 1 small bag
- Tape measure or ruler

gauge
- 6 stitches per inch in stockinette stitch

TIP • If this is your first project in the round, cast all of the stitches onto one double-pointed needle and then distribute the stitches onto the three needles as noted (see p. 4). Also, I suggest starting with one color to simplify.

large squishie

Using three double-pointed needles and the selected yarn, cast on 9 stitches, placing 3 stitches on each needle. Join to knit in the round, being careful not to twist the stitches. Place a stitch marker on the first stitch.

Increase rounds
Round 1 and every odd round: knit
Round 2: kfb in each stitch (6 sts per needle, 18 sts total)
Round 4: repeat (k1, kfb) across round (9 sts per needle, 27 sts total)
Round 6: repeat (k2, kfb) across round (12 sts per needle, 36 sts total)
Round 8: repeat (k3, kfb) across round (15 sts per needle, 45 sts total)
Round 10: repeat (k4, kfb) across round (18 sts per needle, 54 sts total)
Round 12: repeat (k5, kfb) across round (21 sts per needle, 63 sts total)

Place a stitch marker on round 12 and leave it there. Knit every round until the ball measures 2½ inches from the marker.

Decrease rounds
Round 1: repeat (k5, k2tog) across round (18 sts per needle, 54 sts total remain)
Round 2 and every even round: knit
Round 3: repeat (k4, k2tog) across round (15 sts per needle, 45 sts total remain)

Thread the tail on a yarn needle and pass it through the stitches of the cast-on edge. Close up the hole at the bottom of the ball by gathering the stitches. Pull tight and stitch to secure (see p. 16).

After round 4, stuff the ball.

Round 5: repeat (k3, k2tog) across round (12 sts per needle, 36 sts total remain)

Round 7: repeat (k2, k2tog) across round (9 sts per needle, 27 sts total remain)

Round 9: repeat (k1, k2tog) across round (6 sts per needle, 18 sts total remain)

After round 10: finish stuffing the ball so it is firm.

Round 11: repeat (k2tog) across round (3 sts per needle, 9 sts total remain)

Cut the yarn, leaving a 6-inch-long tail, and thread it on a yarn needle. Pull the tail through the remaining stitches, weave to the inside of the ball, and trim.

The samples were worked in the following colors and patterns:

Solid: 1 in Poppy and 1 in Flamingo

stripe pattern

Rounds 1–4: Poppy

Rounds 5–8: Flamingo

Repeat rounds 1–8 to the end. You can end on any round.

single stripe pattern

Rounds 1–18: Lemongrass

Rounds 19–26: Pickle

Rounds 27–32: Lemongrass

Finish the decrease rounds in Lemongrass.

medium squishie

Rounds 1–10: same as for the large ball (18 sts per needle, 54 sts total)

Place a stitch marker on round 10 and leave it there. Knit every round until the ball measures 2 inches from the marker.

Decrease rounds

Rounds 3–12: from the large ball (3 sts per needle, 9 sts total)

Finish the same as for the large ball.

The samples were worked in the following stripe patterns and colors:

Solid: 1 in Lemongrass, 1 in Caribbean

stripe pattern

Rounds 1 and 2: Caribbean

Rounds 3 and 4: Lemongrass

Repeat to the end. You can end on any round.

small squishie

Rounds 1–8: same as for the large ball (15 sts per needle, 45 sts total)

Place a stitch marker on round 8 and leave it there. Knit every round until the ball measures 1½ inches from the marker.

Decrease rounds

Rounds 5–12: from the large ball (3 sts per needle, 9 sts total).

Finish the same as for the large ball.

The samples were worked in the following colors and stripe patterns:

Solid: 1 in Orchid, 1 in Ladybug

stripe pattern

Rounds 1–8: Flamingo

Round 9: Orchid

Round 10: Flamingo

Repeat rounds 9 and 10 four times more (10 rounds total).

Finish decrease rounds in Orchid.

single stripe pattern

Rounds 1–8: Ladybug

Rounds 9–11: Orchid

Rounds 12–14: Ladybug

Finish decrease rounds in Ladybug.

olives

Begin the small Squishie pattern in Pickle. Work to 2 inches above the stitch marker and finish the decrease rounds in Ladybug.

penguin

My kids are especially fond of penguins because they're the team mascot for their summer swim team. Even a brand-new knitter can make this adorable cold-climate friend, because it's made completely out of garter stitch squares. With a fold and a pull and a stitch or two, you'll make your own penguin in a jiffy. Dive right in and give it a try.

finished measurements

- 6 inches tall, 3 inches wide

yarn

- Rowan Pure Wool DK (100% wool; 136 yards/50 grams), 1 skein each #013 Enamel (natural), #003 Anthracite (dark gray), and #035 Quarry (orange)

tools

- U.S. size 5 needles or size needed to obtain gauge
- Polyester fiberfill, 1 small bag
- Poly pellets (optional), 32-ounce bag
- Yarn needle
- Scissors
- Tape measure or ruler
- Pins

gauge

- 6 stitches per inch in stockinette stitch

body

With Enamel, cast on 36 stitches. Work in garter stitch (knit every row) until the piece measures 6 inches from the cast-on edge.

Bind off. Cut the yarn, leaving an 8-inch-long tail, and pull the tail through the remaining stitch. Lay the piece on a table in front of you with the cast-on edge at the left, and the bound-off edge at the right. Fold over 1 inch of the bottom edge and pin down. Whipstitch the fold down. This edge will become the bottom of the penguin.

Fold the cast-on edge to meet the bound-off edge. Whipstitch this edge and the bottom folded edge together, leaving the top open. Fill the body half full with poly pellets and the rest with fiberfill, or fill only with fiberfill. Stuff until firm. Whipstitch the top seam closed.

outer piece

With Anthracite, make another piece as you did for the body.

feet (make 2)

With Quarry, cast on 12 stitches. Knit every row until the foot measures 1 inch from the cast-on edge.

Cut the yarn, leaving a 6-inch-long tail, and thread the tail on a yarn needle. Pull the tail through the 12 stitches and gather tightly. Secure with a knot. Fold the piece in half and whipstitch the edges together. Stuff the foot lightly with fiberfill before closing the last edge. Weave the end to the inside and trim.

neckband

With Quarry, cast on 10 stitches.

Rows 1–4: knit

Bind off. Cut the yarn and pull through the remaining stitch.

finishing

Place the Anthracite square on a table in front of you so one of the corners is facing you as if the piece were diamond-shaped. Place the body in the center of the Anthracite square.

Pull the wings inward and sew them together at the neck for about 1 inch. Tack down the wings to the body using a running stitch (see p. 14) and leaving the corners unattached. The bottom corner folds to the back to make the tail. Tack down the tail to the body using a running stitch.

Pull the top corner over to the front. Stuff the top corner lightly with fiberfill to form the head. Tack down the sides of the beak to the body with a few stitches. The beak remains unattached.

Whipstitch the neckband under the beak and over the front seam. Whipstitch the feet to the bottom front of the body.

eyes

With Enamel and a yarn needle, take 2 small straight stitches (see p. 14) to create the eyes, using the photograph as a guide.

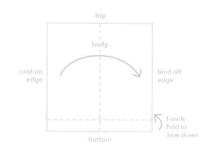

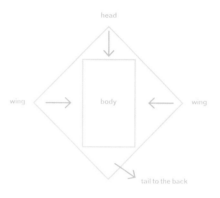

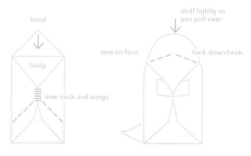

koala mama and baby

My sister collected koala bear toys when she was little. Her stuffed koalas always had a baby hanging on, and the memory of the mama and baby koalas inspired this project.

The koala is a perfect next stepping-stone after the Squishies. The bodies and heads use the same simple pattern as that project, and then you add on to your skills by making the ears and arms. For the long arms, you'll use I-cord, an important skill to master for toy knitting.

This project involves more parts and more stitching together, but it's actually fairly easy to pull together a surefire hit like this.

finished measurements
- Mama: 6 inches tall, 5 inches wide
- Baby: 4 inches tall, 3 inches wide

yarn
- Blue Sky Dyed Cotton (100% organically grown cotton; 150 yards/100 grams), 1 skein each in Stone #626 and Ink #613
- Blue Sky Organic Cotton (100% organic cotton; 150 yards/100 grams), 1 skein in Bone #80

tools
- U.S. size 5 set of four double-pointed needles or size needed to obtain gauge
- Yarn needle
- Polyester fiberfill, 1 small bag
- Scissors
- Tape measure or ruler
- Stitch markers
- Two pairs of Velcro dots
- Sewing needle and thread to match Stone

gauge
- 5½ inches per inch in stockinette stitch

mama koala

body

With Stone, complete as for the large Squishie (see p. 25).

head

With Stone, complete as for the medium Squishie (see p. 26). Whipstitch the head to the body with a length of Stone threaded on a yarn needle. The cast-on end of the head is sewn to the body. Weave the end to the inside and trim.

ears

outer ear (make 2)
With Stone and two double-pointed needles used as straight needles, cast on 7 stitches.
Row 1: knit
Row 2: k1, kfb, k to last 2 sts, kfb, k1 (9 sts)
Rows 3–6: knit
Row 7: repeat row 2 (11 sts)
   Continue knitting every row until the ear measures 2 inches from the cast-on edge.
Decrease row: k1, k2tog, k to the last 3 sts, k2tog, k1 (9 sts remain)
Next row: repeat the decrease row (7 sts remain)
   Bind off. Cut the yarn and pull the end through the remaining stitch.

inner ear (make 2)
With Bone and two double-pointed needles used as straight needles, cast on 5 stitches.
Row 1: knit

Row 2: k1, kfb, k to last 2 sts, kfb, k1 (7 sts)

Rows 3–6: knit

Row 7: repeat row 2 (9 sts)

Continue knitting every row until the inner ear measures 1¾ inches from the cast-on edge.

Decrease row: k1, k2tog, k to last 3 sts, k2tog, k1 (7 sts remain)

Next row: repeat the decrease row (5 sts remain)

Bind off. Cut the yarn and pull the end through the remaining stitch.

finishing

Place each inner ear piece on an outer ear piece, aligning the edges, and whipstitch together using the Bone tail from the bound-off edge threaded on a yarn needle. Whipstitch the ears to the sides of the head, using the Stone tail. Weave the end to the inside and trim.

tummy patch

With Bone, use the outer ear pattern to make the tummy patch. Whipstitch to the body using the Bone tail threaded on a yarn needle and the photograph as a guide. Weave the end to the inside and trim.

arms and hands (make 2)

With Stone and two double-pointed needles used as straight needles, cast on 4 stitches. Work in I-cord (see p. 7) until the arm measures 5½ inches from the cast-on edge.

Continue on to create the hands:

Row 1: kfb, k2, kfb (6 sts)

Row 2: kfb in each stitch, and change to working in the round by transferring 4 stitches onto each of three double-pointed needles (4 sts per needle, 12 sts total)

Place a stitch marker on the first stitch and begin working in the round. Knit every round until the hand measures 1 inch from the first round.

Next round: (k2, k2tog), repeat to end of round (3 sts per needle, 9 sts total remain)

Cut the yarn, leaving a short tail, and thread on a yarn needle. Pull through the remaining stitches and pull up tight to close the hole. Weave the end to the inside, stitch to secure, and trim.

Using the tail from the cast-on stitches and a yarn needle, whipstitch the arms to the sides of the body.

With a sewing needle and matching thread, sew Velcro dots to the palms of the hands, attaching one hook dot to one palm and one loop dot to the other.

feet (make 2)

With Stone, cast on 12 stitches, placing 4 stitches on each of three double-pointed needles. Join to work in the round, being careful not to twist the stitches. Place a stitch marker on the first stitch.

Knit every round until the foot measures 1 inch from the cast-on edge.

Next round: (k2, k2tog), repeat to end of round (3 sts per needle, 9 sts total remain)

Thread the tail from the cast-on stitches on a yarn needle, gather the stitches to close the hole, and stitch to secure. Weave the end to the inside and trim. Stuff the foot lightly with fiberfill.

Cut the yarn, leaving a 6-inch-long tail, and thread on a yarn needle. Pull through the remaining stitches and pull up tight to close the hole. Whipstitch the feet to the bottom of the body with a yarn needle.

fingers and toes, optional (make 12 total)

With Ink and two double-pointed needles used as straight needles, cast on 2 stitches. Work in I-cord until the cord measures ½ inch from the cast-on edge.

Next row: k2tog (1 st remains)

Cut the yarn and pull through the last stitch. Attach 3 fingers and 3 toes on each hand and foot with a yarn needle and a few stitches. Weave ends to the inside and trim.

nose

With Ink and two double-pointed needles used as straight needles, cast on 3 stitches. Work in I-cord until the nose measures ½ inch from the cast-on edge. Bind off. Cut the yarn and pull through the remaining stitch. Whipstitch the nose to the center of the face using the bound-off tail threaded on a yarn needle.

eyes and mouth

With a yarn needle and a length of Ink, embroider the face using straight stitches (see p. 14) and the photograph as a guide.

baby koala

body

With Stone, complete as for the small Squishie (see p. 26).

head

With Stone, follow the large Squishie pattern (see p. 25) as follows:

Increase rounds

Complete rounds 1–6 (12 sts per needle, 36 sts total).

Place a stitch marker on round 6 and leave it there. Knit every round until the head measures 1 inch from the stitch marker.

Decrease rounds

Complete rounds 7–11.

Whipstitch the cast-on end of the head to the body with a yarn needle. Weave the end to the inside and trim. The baby's face should look to the side.

ears

outer ear (make 2)

With Stone and two double-pointed needles used as straight needles, cast on 7 stitches. Knit every row until the ear measures 1 inch from the cast-on edge.
Next row: k1, k2tog,k1, k2tog, k1 (5 sts remain)

Bind off. Cut the yarn and pull through the remaining stitch.

inner ear (make 2)

With Bone and two double-pointed needles used as straight needles, cast on 5 stitches. Knit every row until the ear measures ¾ inch from the cast-on edge.
Next row: k2tog, k1, k2tog (3 sts remain)

Bind off. Cut the yarn and pull through the remaining stitch.

finishing

Place each inner ear piece on an outer ear piece, aligning the edges, and whipstitch together using the Bone tail from the bind off threaded on a yarn needle. Whipstitch the ears to the sides of the head with the Stone tail. Weave the end to the inside and trim.

tummy patch

With Bone and two double-pointed needles used as straight needles, cast on 5 stitches.
Row 1: knit
Row 2: k1, kfb, k1, kfb, k1 (7 sts)

Knit every row until the patch measures 1½ inches from the cast-on edge.
Next row: k1, k2tog, k1, k2tog, k1 (5 sts remain)

Bind off. Cut the yarn and pull through the remaining stitch.

Whipstitch the tummy patch to the body using a yarn needle.

arms and hands (make 2)

With Stone and two double-pointed needles used as straight needles, cast on 3 stitches. Work in I-cord until the arm measures 4½ inches from the cast-on edge.
Next row: kfb in each stitch (6 sts)

Place 2 stitches on each of three double-pointed needles. Begin working in the round. Place a stitch marker on the first stitch.
Next round: (k1, kfb), repeat on each needle (3 sts per needle, 9 sts total)

Knit every round until the hand measures ¾ inch from the first round.
Next round: (k1, k2tog), repeat on each needle (2 sts per needle, 6 sts total)

Cut the yarn, leaving a 6-inch-long tail, and thread on a yarn needle. Pull through the remaining stitches, gather up tight to close the hole, and stitch to secure. Weave the end to the inside and trim. Whipstitch the arms to the body with the tail from the cast-on stitches threaded on a yarn needle.

With a sewing needle and matching thread, sew Velcro dots to the palms of the hands, attaching one hook dot to one palm and one loop dot to the other.

feet (make 2)

With Stone, cast on 9 stitches, placing 3 stitches on each of three double-pointed needles. Join to knit in the round, being careful not to twist the stitches. Place a stitch marker on the first stitch. Knit every round until the foot measures 1 inch from the cast-on stitches.

Next round: (k1, k2tog) on each needle (2 sts per needle, 6 sts total)

Thread the tail from the cast-on stitches on a yarn needle and stitch through the cast-on stitches, gathering them up to close the hole. Stuff the foot lightly with fiberfill. Cut the yarn, leaving a 6-inch-long tail, and thread on a yarn needle. Pull the tail through the remaining stitches and gather up tight to close the hole. With a yarn needle and the tails from the cast-on stitches, whipstitch the feet to the bottom of the body.

fingers and toes, optional (make 12 total)

With Ink and two double-pointed needles used as straight needles, cast on 2 stitches. Work in I-cord for 2 rows.

Next row: k2tog

Cut the yarn and pull through the remaining stitch. Sew 3 toes and fingers to each foot and hand using the yarn needle and the tails from the cast-on edges. Weave ends to the inside and trim.

nose

With Ink and two double-pointed needles used as straight needles, cast on 3 sts. Work in I-cord until the nose measures ¼ inch from the cast-on edge.

Bind off. Cut the yarn and pull through the remaining stitch. Using a yarn needle and a length of Ink, whipstitch the nose to the center of the face, using the photograph as a guide.

eyes and mouth

With a length of Ink and a yarn needle, embroider the eyes and mouth using straight stitches and the photograph as a guide.

3

animal friends

There is a depth of craftsmanship to handknit plush toys that you don't find in store-bought versions. The love, care, and effort it takes to craft these handmade animal toys make a huge difference. With the skills you learned in the last chapter, I'm sure you'll be able to make these sweet animal friends. All of them will bring a smile to a child's face, and each one is an undeniable treasure. A bunny and a pig make perfect friends, and an itty-bitty lamb and a large-size giraffe finish off the chapter with lovable style. The fun has just begun, so let's get busy and knit.

bunny

"I'm late, I'm late, for a very important date!" Actually, you won't fret like the White Rabbit if you create this lovable toy for a child's special day. It's quite simple, and will work up just in time to be given as a cherished gift.

Plush toy bunnies fascinate me in every way because the options are endless. This lovable version of the basic bunny has fantastic features, including long legs and arms, big funny paws, a little potbelly, and a sweet, minimal face.

finished measurements

- 8 inches tall when seated, 4½ inches wide

yarn

- Blue Sky Dyed Cotton (100% organically grown cotton; 150 yards/100 grams), 2 skeins in Tulip #615, 1 skein in Shell #606

tools

- U.S. size 5 set of four double-pointed needles, or size needed to obtain gauge
- Yarn needle
- Polyester fiberfill, 1 small bag
- Poly pellets (optional), 32-ounce bag
- Stitch markers
- Scissors
- Tape measure or ruler
- Black embroidery floss

gauge

- 5½ stitches per inch in stockinette stitch

body

With Tulip, cast on 9 stitches, placing 3 stitches on each of three double-pointed needles. Join to work in the round, being careful not to twist the stitches. Place a stitch marker on the first stitch.

Round 1: knit

Round 2: kfb in each stitch (6 sts per needle, 18 sts total)

Round 3: knit

Round 4: kfb in each stitch (12 sts per needle, 36 sts total)

Rounds 5–7: knit

Round 8: (k2, kfb), repeat to end of round (16 sts per needle, 48 sts total)

Round 9: knit

Round 10: (k3, kfb), repeat to end of round (20 sts per needle, 60 sts total)

Rounds 11 and 12: knit

Round 13: purl

Continue to knit every round until the body measures 3 inches from the purl round.

Decrease rounds

Round 1: (k3, k2tog), repeat to end of round (16 sts per needle, 48 sts total remain)

Rounds 2–6: knit

Round 7: (k2, k2tog), repeat to end of round (12 sts per needle, 36 sts total remain)

Rounds 8–12: knit

Round 13: (k1, k2tog), repeat to end of round (8 sts per needle, 24 sts total remain)

Rounds 14–18: knit

Thread the tail from the cast-on stitches on a yarn needle. Stitch through all of the cast-on stitches, pull up tight to close the hole in the

Round 4: (k1, k2tog), repeat to end of round (8 sts per needle, 24 sts total remain)

Rounds 5 and 6: knit

Thread the tail from the cast-on stitches on a yarn needle. Stitch through all of the cast-on stitches and gather to close the hole on the back of the head. Stitch to secure. Weave the end to the inside and trim.

Stuff the head with fiberfill.

Round 7: (k2tog), repeat to end of round (4 sts per needle, 12 sts total remain)

Round 8: (k1, k2tog, k1), repeat on each needle (3 sts per needle, 9 sts remain)

Finish stuffing. Cut the yarn, leaving a 6-inch-long tail, and thread on a yarn needle. Pull through the remaining stitches, gather up tight to close the hole, and stitch to secure. Weave the end to the inside and trim.

With the tail from the body threaded on a yarn needle, whipstitch the head to the body. Weave the tail to the inside and trim.

ears

outer ear (make 2)

With Tulip and two double-pointed needles used as straight needles, cast on 11 stitches.

Work in stockinette stitch (knit 1 row, purl 1 row) until the ear measures 3 inches from the cast-on edge, ending with a purl row.

Decrease rows

Row 1: k1, ssk, k5, k2tog, k1 (9 sts remain)

Row 2: purl

Row 3: k1, ssk, k3, k2tog, k1 (7 sts remain)

Row 4: purl

Row 5: k1, ssk, k1, k2tog, k1 (5 sts remain)

Row 6: p2tog, p1, p2tog (3 sts remain)

Bind off. Cut the yarn, leaving an 8-inch-long tail, and pull through the remaining stitch.

inner ear (make 2)

With Shell and two double-pointed needles used as straight needles, cast on 9 stitches.

bottom, and stitch to secure. Weave the end to the inside and trim. Fill one-third full with poly pellets and stuff the rest with fiberfill or fill with fiberfill only.

Round 19: (k2tog), repeat to end of round (4 sts per needle, 12 sts total remain)

Round 20: (k1, k2tog, k1), repeat on each needle (3 sts per needle, 9 sts total remain)

Finish stuffing. Cut the yarn, leaving an 8-inch-long tail, and thread on a yarn needle. Pull through the remaining stitches, gather up tight to close the hole, and stitch to secure. Leave the tail free to use later to attach the head.

head

Starting at the back of the head, with Tulip, work the same as for the body through round 8 (16 sts per needle, 48 sts total remain).

Knit every round for 14 rounds.

Decrease rounds

Round 1: (k2, k2tog), repeat to end of round (12 sts per needle, 36 sts total remain)

Rounds 2 and 3: knit

Work in stockinette stitch until the inner ear measures 3 inches from the cast-on edge, ending with a purl row.

Decrease rows
Row 1: k1, ssk, k3, k2tog, k1 (7 sts remain)
Row 2: purl
Row 3: k1, ssk, k1, k2tog, k1 (5 sts remain)
Row 4: p2tog, p1, p2tog (3 sts remain)
Bind off. Cut the yarn and pull through the remaining stitch.

finishing
Place each inner ear piece on an outer ear piece, purl sides together. Whipstitch the pieces together using the tails from the outer ears threaded on a yarn needle.

Attach the ears to the head with the inner ear facing downward, using the photograph as a guide.

face
With a yarn needle and black embroidery floss, take two tiny straight stitches (see p. 14) to create each eye and use longer straight stitches for the nose, using the photograph as a guide.

arms (make 2)
With Tulip, cast on 15 stitches, placing 5 stitches on each of three double-pointed needles. Join to work in the round, being careful not to twist the stitches. Place a stitch marker on the first stitch.

Knit every round until the arm measures 3 inches from the cast-on edge.
Next round: (k2, m1, k3) on each needle (6 sts per needle, 18 sts total)

Continue to knit every round until the arm measures 4 inches from the cast-on edge.
Next round: k1, m1, k7, m1, k1, m1, k8, m1, k1 (22 sts total)
Needles 1 and 3: 7 sts
Needle 2: 8 sts

Knit every round until the arm measures 5 inches from the cast-on edge.

Finish the paw:
Round 1:
Needle 1: k to last 2 sts, k2tog (6 sts remain)
Needle 2: k2tog, k to last 2 sts, k2tog (6 sts remain)
Needle 3: same as needle 1 (6 sts remain)
(6 sts per needle, 18 sts total remain)
Round 2: (k1, k2tog), repeat to end of round
(4 sts per needle, 12 sts total remain)
Round 3: knit
Round 4: (k2tog), repeat to end of round
(2 sts per needle, 6 sts total remain)

Cut the yarn, leaving a 6-inch-long tail, and thread on a yarn needle. Pull through the remaining stitches, gather up tight to close the hole, and stitch to secure. Weave the end to the inside and trim.

Fill the paw with poly pellets and stuff the rest of the arm with fiberfill, or stuff with fiberfill only. Whipstitch the top of the arm closed with a yarn needle. Attach the arms to the sides of the body, using the photograph as a guide.

With black embroidery floss and a yarn needle, take three stitches through the paw, using the photograph as a guide. Secure, weave the end to the inside, and trim.

legs (make 2)
With Tulip, cast on 15 stitches, placing 5 stitches on each of three double-pointed needles. Join to work in the round, being careful not to twist the stitches. Place a stitch marker on the first stitch.

Knit every round until the leg measures 5 inches from the cast-on edge. Bind off. Cut the yarn, leaving a 6-inch-long tail, and pull the end through the remaining stitch.

feet (make 2)
With Tulip, cast on 6 stitches, placing 2 stitches on each of three double-pointed needles. Join to work in the round, being careful not to twist the stitches. Place a stitch marker on the first stitch.
Round 1: knit
Round 2: (k1, m1, k1), repeat on each needle (3 sts per needle, 9 sts total)
Round 3: knit

Round 4: (k1, m1, k1, m1, k1), repeat on each needle (5 sts per needle, 15 sts total)

Round 5: knit

Round 6: (k1, m1, k3, m1, k1), repeat on each needle (7 sts per needle, 21 sts total)

Knit every round for 15 rounds.

Decrease rounds

Round 1: (k1, k2tog, k4), repeat on each needle (6 sts per needle, 18 sts total)

Round 2: ssk, k8, k2tog, k6 (16 sts total remain)

Divide the stitches, placing 8 stitches on each of two double-pointed needles. Cut the yarn, leaving an 8-inch-long tail, and thread on a yarn needle. Fill the foot with poly pellets or fiberfill. Use kitchener stitch (see p. 9) to graft the toe. Weave the end to the inside and trim.

Whipstitch the feet to the bound-off edges of the legs with the tails from the legs and a yarn needle. Stuff the legs with fiberfill. Whipstitch to the bottom front of the body with a yarn needle, using the photograph as a guide

With a yarn needle and black embroidery floss take three stitches through each foot, as shown in the photograph. Secure, weave to the inside, and trim.

tail

With Tulip, make a 2-inch pom-pom with 40 wraps. Use the ends from the tie and a yarn needle to attach it to the rear lower center of the body.

pig

"This little piggy went to market, this little piggy stayed home . . ." I am so glad this piggy stayed at my home because he is too cute for words, simultaneously sweet and funny.

You shape the pig's curly tail by placing a pipe cleaner inside I-cord and then giving it a swirl—a simple trick that's a fun addition to your toy-knitting repertoire. Add easy construction and minimal seams, and it's a cinch to knit your own little piggy to take to market, or anywhere else.

finished measurements

· 8 inches tall when seated, 4½ inches wide

yarn

· Blue Sky Dyed Cotton (100% organically dyed cotton; 150 yards/100 grams), 2 skeins in Shell #606 and a small amount of Sand #81

tools

· U.S. size 5 set of four double-pointed needles, or size needed to obtain gauge
· Scissors
· Yarn needle
· Stitch markers
· Polyester fiberfill, 1 small bag
· Poly pellets (optional), 32-ounce bag
· Black embroidery floss
· Tape measure or ruler
· Stitch holder
· Pink pipe cleaner

gauge

· 5½ stitches per inch in stockinette stitch

body

With Shell, cast on 9 stitches, placing 3 stitches on each of three double-pointed needles. Join to work in the round, being careful not to twist the stitches. Place a stitch marker on the first stitch.

Round 1: knit

Round 2: kfb in each stitch (6 sts per needle, 18 sts total)

Round 3: knit

Round 4: kfb in each stitch (12 sts per needle, 36 sts total)

Rounds 5–7: knit

Round 8: (k2, kfb), repeat to end of round (16 sts per needle, 48 sts total)

Round 9: knit

Round 10: (k3, kfb), repeat to end of round (20 sts per needle, 60 sts total)

Rounds 11 and 12: knit

Place a stitch marker on round 12 and leave it there. Knit every round until the body measures 3 inches from the stitch marker.

Decrease rounds

Round 1: (k3, k2tog), repeat to end of round (16 sts per needle, 48 sts total remain)

Rounds 2–6: knit

Round 7: (k2, k2tog), repeat to end of round (12 sts per needle, 36 sts total remain)

Rounds 8–12: knit

Round 13: k1, k2tog, repeat to end of round (8 sts per needle, 24 sts total remain)

Rounds 14–18: knit

Thread the tail from the cast-on stitches on a yarn needle. Stitch through all of the cast-on stitches, pull tight to close the hole on the bottom, and stitch to secure. Weave the end to the inside and trim.

Fill the body one-third full with poly pellets and stuff the rest with fiberfill, or fill with fiberfill only.

Round 19: (k2tog), repeat to end of round (4 sts per needle, 12 sts total remain)
Round 20: (k1, k2tog, k1), repeat on each needle (3 sts per needle, 9 sts total remain)

Finish stuffing the body. Cut the yarn, leaving a 6-inch-long tail, and thread the end on a yarn needle. Pull through the remaining stitches, gather up tight to close the hole, and stitch to secure. Leave the tail free to use later for attaching the head.

head

Starting at the back of the head, with Shell, work the same as for the body through round 8 (16 sts per needle, 48 sts total remain).

Knit every round for 14 rounds.

Decrease rounds
Round 1: k2, k2tog, repeat to end of round (12 sts per needle, 36 sts total)
Round 2: (k1, k2tog), repeat to end of round (8 sts per needle, 24 sts total)
Rounds 3–12: knit

Thread the tail from the cast-on stitches on a yarn needle. Sew through all of the cast-on stitches, pull up tight to close the hole in the back of the head, and stitch to secure. Stuff the head with fiberfill. Continue to fill the head as you work.
Round 13: (k2tog), repeat to end of round (4 sts per needle, 12 sts total)
Round 14: (k1, k2tog, k1), repeat on each needle (3 sts per needle, 9 sts total)

Cut the yarn, leaving a 6-inch tail, and thread on a yarn needle. Stuff the remainder of the head, pull the tail through the remaining stitches, and pull up tight to close the hole, stitching to secure. Weave the end to the inside and trim.

tip of snout

With Sand and two double-pointed needles used as straight needles, cast on 3 stitches.
Row 1: kfb, k1, kfb (5 sts)
Row 2: purl
Row 3: knit
Row 4: purl
Row 5: ssk, k1, k2tog

Bind off. Cut the yarn, leaving a 6-inch-long tail, and pull through the remaining stitch. Thread the end on a yarn needle and whipstitch the tip to the end of the snout. Weave the end to the inside and trim.

With a yarn needle and the tail from the top of the body, whipstitch the head to the body. Weave the end to the inside and trim.

ears (make 4)

With Shell and two double-pointed needles used as straight needles, cast on 11 stitches. Work in stockinette stitchknit 1 row, purl 1 row until the ear measures 1½ inches from the cast-on edge, ending with a purl row.

Decrease rows
Row 1: k1, ssk, k5, k2tog, k1 (9 sts remain)
Row 2: purl
Row 3: k1, ssk, k3, k2tog, k1 (7 sts remain)
Row 4: purl
Row 5: k1, ssk, k1, k2tog, k1 (5 sts remain)
Row 6: purl
Row 7: k1, ssk, k2tog (3 sts remain)
Row 8: purl
Row 9: k1, k2tog, pass the first stitch over the second and off the needle (1 st remains)

Cut the yarn and pull through the remaining stitch.

finishing

Place 2 ear pieces together, purl sides facing and edges aligned. With a yarn needle and the tail, whipstitch the edges of the ear pieces together. Repeat for second ear. Whipstitch the ears to the head, folding in the bottom corners and using the photograph as a guide.

eyes and nostrils

With the black embroidery floss and the yarn needle, take two small straight stitches (see p. 14) for each eye, using the photograph as a guide. Take two small straight stitches for the nostrils. Weave the ends to the inside and trim.

arms (make 2)

With Shell, cast on 15 stitches, placing 5 stitches on each of three double-pointed needles. Join to work in the round, being careful not to twist the stitches. Place a stitch marker on the first stitch.

Knit every round until the arm measures 3 inches from the cast-on edge.

Next round: (k2, m1, k3) on each needle (6 sts per needle, 18 sts total)

Continue to knit every round until the arm measures 4 inches from the cast-on edge.

Next round: k1, m1, k7, m1, k1, m1, k8, m1, k1 (22 sts total)

Needles 1 and 3: 7 sts

Needle 2: 8 sts

Knit every round until the arm measures 4½ inches from the cast-on edge.

Next round: k across 11 sts. Place the other 11 stitches on a stitch holder. Arrange the first 11 stitches on three double-pointed needles as follows:

Needles 1 and 2: 4 sts

Needle 3: 3 sts

Rounds 1–3: knit

Round 4: (k2tog), repeat to last stitch, k1 (6 sts remain)

Cut the yarn, leaving a 6-inch-long tail, and thread on a yarn needle. Pull through the remaining stitches, gather up tight to close the hole, and stitch to secure.

Arrange the stitches from the yarn holder back on the three double-pointed needles as set out in the last step. Reattach the yarn to the last stitch you knit, and complete the second side the same way as the first. Sew the gap in the middle of the two groups of stitches closed with a few whipstitches. Fill the hand with poly pellets and the arm with fiberfill, or with fiberfill only.

With the yarn from the cast-on edge threaded on a yarn needle, whipstitch the top of the arm closed. Whipstitch the arms to the sides of the body, using the photograph as a guide.

legs (make 2)

With Shell, cast on 18 stitches, placing 6 stitches on each of three double-pointed needles. Join to work in the round, being careful not to twist the stitches. Place a stitch marker on the first stitch.

Knit every round until the leg measures 4 inches from the cast-on edge. Bind off. Cut the yarn and pull through the remaining stitch.

feet (make 2)

With Shell, cast on 6 stitches, placing 2 stitches on each of three double-pointed needles. Join to work in the round, being careful not to twist the stitches. Place a stitch marker on the first stitch.

Round 1: knit

Round 2: (k1, m1, k1), repeat on each needle (3 sts per needle, 9 sts total)

Round 3: knit

Round 4: (k1, m1, k1, m1, k1), repeat on each needle (5 sts per needle, 15 sts total)

Round 5: knit

Round 6:

Needles 1 and 2: (k1, m1, k3, m1, k1), repeat on each needle (7 sts per needle)

Needle 3: k1, m1, k3, m1, k1 (8 sts)

22 total stitches

Rounds 7–15: knit

Thread the tail from the cast-on edge stitches on a yarn needle. Stitch through all of the stitches in the cast-on row, gather, and stitch to secure. Fill the foot with poly pellets or stuff with fiberfill.

Next round: k across 11 sts. Place the other 11 stitches on a stitch holder. Arrange the first 11 stitches on three double-pointed needles as follows:

Needles 1 and 2: 4 sts

Needle 3: 3 sts

Rounds 1–3: knit

Finish filling or stuffing.

Round 4: (k2tog), repeat to last stitch, k1 (6 sts remain)

Cut the yarn, leaving a 6-inch-long tail, and thread on a yarn needle. Pull through the remaining stitches, gather tightly, and take a few stitches to close the hole.

Arrange the stitches from the yarn holder back on the three double-pointed needles as set out in the last step. Reattach the yarn to the last stitch you knit, and complete the second side the same way as the first. Sew the gap in the middle of the two groups of stitches closed with a few whipstitches.

Whipstitch the feet to the leg using the tail from the bound-off edge and a yarn needle. Stuff the legs with fiberfill. Whipstitch the legs to the body with the tail from the cast-on edge, using the photograph as a guide.

tail

With Shell and two double-pointed needles used as straight needles, cast on 4 stitches. Work in I-cord (see p. 7) until the tail measures 5 inches from the cast-on edge. Bind off. Cut the yarn and pull through the remaining stitch.

Cut the pipe cleaner to measure 4¾ inches. Fold over both ends of the pipe cleaner and push it into the center of the I-cord. Sew both ends of the I-cord closed with a couple of stitches. Attach one end of the tail to the lower center back of the body. Spiral the tail around a knitting needle to create a corkscrew curl.

lamb

Every knitter loves a knitted lamb. The boucle yarn used for the body and the curly topknot are perfect for creating that wooly look. The legs are cleverly constructed of I-cords stuffed with straws, which allow the lamb to stand on its own. Make one for your favorite child and another for your favorite knitter—they'll both love it.

finished measurements

- 6½ inches tall when standing, 5 inches long, front to back

yarn

- Debbie Bliss Cashmerino Astrakhan (60% wool, 30% microfiber, 10% cashmere; 77 yards/50 grams), 1 skein in Off-White #3
- Blue Sky Organic Cotton (100% organic cotton; 150 yards/100 grams), 1 skein in Sand #81

tools

- U.S. size 4 set of four double-pointed needles, or size needed to obtain gauge
- Yarn needle
- Scissors
- Tape measure or ruler
- Stitch marker
- Black embroidery floss
- Polyester fiberfill, 1 small bag
- Poly pellets (optional), 32-ounce bag
- 1 drinking straw

gauge

- 6 sts per inch in stockinette stitch for the body

back end

With Off-White and two double-pointed needles used as straight needles, cast on 4 stitches.

Row 1: kfb, k to last stitch, kfb (6 sts)
Row 2: pfb, p to last stitch, pfb (8 sts)
Rows 3 and 4: repeat rows 1 and 2 (12 sts)

Work in stockinette stitch (knit one row, purl one row) until the back end measures 2 inches from the cast-on edge, ending with a purl row.

Decrease rows

Row 1: ssk, k to last 2 stitches, k2tog (10 sts remain)
Row 2: p2tog, p to last 2 stitches, p2tog (8 sts remain)
Rows 3 and 4: repeat rows 1 and 2 (4 sts remain)

body

Continue on from the back end:

Knit the 4 stitches on the needle, then on the same needle pick up 10 stitches (see p. 8), on a second double-pointed needle pick up 14 stitches, and on a third double-pointed needle pick up 14 stitches. (14 sts per needle, 42 sts total)

Place a stitch marker on the first stitch, and begin working in the round.

Increase round: (kfb, k to the last stitch, kfb), repeat on each needle (16 sts per needle, 48 sts total)
Next round: repeat the increase round (18 sts per needle, 54 sts total)

Knit every round until the body measures 2 inches above the pickup round.

Decrease rounds

Round 1: (k7, k2tog), repeat to end of round (16 sts per needle, 48 sts total remain)
Rounds 2–5: knit
Round 6: (k6, k2tog), repeat to end of round (14 sts per needle, 42 sts total remain)
Round 7: (k5, k2tog), repeat to end of round (12 sts per needle, 36 sts total remain)
Rounds 8 and 9: knit
Round 10: (k4, k2tog), repeat to end of round (10 sts per needle, 30 sts total remain)
Round 11: (k3, k2tog), repeat to end of round (8 sts per needle, 24 sts total remain)
Round 12: knit
Round 13: (k2, k2tog), repeat to end of round (6 sts per needle, 18 sts total remain)

Holding the body horizontally, pour a layer of poly pellets into the bottom, fill the top with fiberfill, or stuff with fiberfill only.

Round 14: (k1, k2tog), repeat to end of round (4 sts per needle, 12 sts total remain)

Round 15: k2tog, repeat to end of round (2 sts per needle, 6 sts total remain)

Finish stuffing. Cut the yarn, leaving a 6-inch-long tail, and thread the tail on a yarn needle. Pull the end through the remaining stitches, gather up tight to close the hole, and stitch to secure. Weave the end to the inside and trim.

tail

With Off-White, cast on 12 stitches, placing 4 stitches on each of three double-pointed needles. Join to work in the round, being careful not to twist the stitches. Place a stitch marker on the first stitch.

Knit every round until the tail measures ½ inch from the cast-on edge.

Decrease rounds

Round 1: (k2, k2tog), repeat on each needle (3 sts per needle, 9 sts total remain)

Round 2: (k1, k2tog), repeat on each needle (2 sts per needle, 6 sts total remain)

Round 3: (k2tog), repeat on each needle (1 st per needle, 3 sts total remain)

Cut the yarn, leaving a 6-inch-long tail, and thread on a yarn needle. Pull the end through the remaining stitches, gather up tight to close the hole, and stitch to secure. Weave the end to the inside and trim. Thread the tail from the cast-on edge on a yarn needle. Whipstitch the tail to the top of the back end. Weave the end to the inside and trim.

legs (make 4)

With Sand and two double-pointed needles used as straight needles, cast on 4 stitches. Work in I-cord (see p. 7) until the leg measures 1 inch from the cast-on edge. Bind off. Cut the yarn and pull through the remaining stitch.

Cut the drinking straw to fit inside of the I-cord. Push the straw inside of the I-cord and set aside.

feet (make 4)

With Sand, cast on 9 stitches, placing 3 stitches on each of three double-pointed needles. Join to work in the round, being careful not to twist the stitches. Place a stitch marker on the first stitch.

Round 1: knit

Round 2: (k1, m1, k1, m1, k1), repeat on each needle (5 sts per needle, 15 sts total)

Rounds 3–7: knit

Round 8: (k3, k2tog), repeat on each needle (4 sts per needle, 12 sts total remain)

Thread the tail from the cast-on stitches on a yarn needle. Stitch through all of the stitches in the cast-on row and gather up, pulling tight to close the hole. Stitch to secure. Fill the foot with poly pellets or stuff with fiberfill. The foot is supposed to be flat, not rounded.

Round 9: (k2, k2tog), repeat on each needle (3 sts per needle, 9 sts total remain)

Round 10: (k1, k2tog), repeat on each needle (2 sts per needle, 6 sts total remain)

Cut the yarn, leaving a 6-inch-long tail, and thread on a yarn needle. Pull through the remaining stitches, gather up tight to close the hole, and stitch to secure. Weave the end to the inside and trim.

Whipstitch the feet to the back top of the legs with the cast-on tail from the legs threaded on a yarn needle, using the photograph as a guide. Whipstitch the leg to the bottom of the body, using the bound-off tail threaded on a yarn needle.

head

With Sand, cast on 9 stitches, placing 3 stitches on each of three double-pointed needles. Join to work in the round, being careful not to twist the stitches. Place a stitch marker on the first stitch.

Round 1: knit
Round 2: (k1, m1, k1, m1, k1), repeat on each needle (5 sts per needle, 15 sts total)
Rounds 3 and 4: knit
Round 5: (k1, [k1, m1] four times), repeat on each needle (9 sts per needle, 27 sts total)
Rounds 6–15: knit
Round 16: (ssk, k5, k2tog), repeat on each needle (7 sts per needle, 21 sts total remain)
Rounds 17 and 18: knit
Round 19: (ssk, k3, k2tog), repeat on each needle (5 sts per needle, 15 sts total remain)
Round 20: knit
Round 21: (k3, k2tog), repeat on each needle (4 sts per needle, 12 sts total remain)

Thread the tail from the cast-on stitches on a yarn needle. Stitch through all of the cast-on stitches, pull up tight to close the hole, and stitch to secure. Begin to stuff the head with fiberfill.

Round 22: (k2, k2tog), repeat on each needle (3 sts per needle, 9 sts total remain)

Finish stuffing. Cut the yarn, leaving a 6-inch-long tail, and thread the end on a yarn needle. Pull the end through the remaining stitches, gather up tight to close the hole, and stitch to secure. This is the nose end of the head. Pull the tail through to the bottom side of the head and whipstitch to the front top of the body, using the photo as a guide.

ears (make 2)

With Sand, cast on 6 stitches, placing 2 stitches on each of three double-pointed needles. Join to work in the round, being careful not to twist the stitches. Place a stitch marker on the first stitch.

Rounds 1–4: knit
Round 5: (k1, m1, k1), repeat on each needle (3 sts per needle, 9 sts total)
Rounds 6–9: knit
Round 10: (k1, k2tog), repeat on each needle (2 sts per needle, 6 sts total remain)
Round 11: knit

Cut the yarn, leaving a 6-inch-long tail, and thread the end on a yarn needle. Pull the end through the remaining stitches, pull up tight to close the hole, and stitch to secure. Weave the end to the inside and trim. Thread the tail from the cast-on stitches on a yarn needle. Whipstitch the ears to the head, using the photograph as a guide.

hair

With Off-White and two double-pointed needles used as straight needles, cast on 4 stitches and begin to work in twisted loop stitch.

Row 1: complete the twisted loop stitch in every stitch, as follows:

Knit the stitch and leave it on the left needle. Pull the loop that is on the right needle out about 2 inches. Transfer the loop onto your right index finger. Twist the loop in one direction until it folds back on itself.

Place the loop back on the left needle.
Knit the two stitches together.
Row 2: purl
Row 3: repeat row 1
Row 4: p2tog twice (2 sts remain)

Bind off. Cut the yarn and pull through the last stitch, leaving a 6-inch-long tail. Thread the tail on a yarn needle and whipstitch the hair to the top of the head between the ears. Weave the end to the inside and trim.

face and toes

With black embroidery floss and a yarn needle, create the eyes with 2 small straight stitches each (see p. 14). Create the nose with straight stitches. On each foot, take a stitch at the center front of the foot, stitching over and under the foot, using the photograph as a guide.

giraffe

"I can put them on a cat and I can put them on a hat." That's what Robert Lopshire wrote about spots in *Put Me in the Zoo*. I can and have put spots on just about everything I knit, and here I've used them on a friendly giraffe. It's big—more than 20 inches tall! That size gives it a substantial, snuggly feel.

There are many fun details in the design, including appliqué spots and a pom-pom mane. With this project, you can do it all or pick and choose what you want to add. I suggest taking the time to do every last spot; it will be well worth your while.

finished measurements

- 14 inches tall when seated, 7½ inches wide

yarn

- Cascade Yarns 220 Superwash (100% superwash wool; 220 yards/100 grams), 2 skeins in Daffodil #821, 1 skein in Orange #825

tools

- U.S. size 5 set of four double-pointed needles, or size needed to obtain gauge
- U.S. size 5 12-inch circular needle, or size needed to obtain gauge (optional)
- Scissors
- Yarn needle
- Polyester fiberfill, 1 small bag
- Poly pellets (optional), 32-ounce bag
- Tape measure or ruler
- Pins
- Stitch markers
- Small amount of worsted-weight brown yarn for embroidering the face
- 1 drinking straw

gauge

- 6 stitches per inch in stockinette stitch

body

With Daffodil and double-pointed needles, cast on 9 stitches, placing 3 stitches on each of three needles. Join to work in the round, being careful not to twist the stitches. Place a stitch marker on the first stitch.

Round 1: knit

Round 2: kfb in each stitch (6 sts per needle, 18 sts total)

Round 3: knit

Round 4: kfb in each stitch (12 sts per needle, 36 sts total)

Rounds 5–7: knit

Round 8: (k2, kfb), repeat to end of round (16 sts per needle, 48 sts total)

Round 9: knit

Round 10: (k3, kfb), repeat to end of round (20 sts per needle, 60 sts total)

Rounds 11–13: knit

Round 14: (k4, kfb), repeat to end of round (24 sts per needle, 72 sts total)

Rounds 15–17: knit

Round 18: (k5, kfb), repeat to end of round (28 sts per needle, 84 sts total)

Rounds 19–21: knit

Round 22: (k6, kfb), repeat to end of round (32 sts per needle, 96 sts total)

Place a stitch marker on round 22 and leave it there.

Either continue on the double-pointed needles or knit onto a 12-inch circular needle. Knit every round until the body measures 4 inches from the stitch marker.

Decrease rounds for neck

Round 1: (k6, k2tog), repeat to end of round (28 sts per needle if working on double-pointed needles, 84 sts total remain)

Round 2: (k5, k2tog), repeat to end of round (24 sts per needle if working on double-pointed needles, 72 sts total remain)

Rounds 3–14: knit (If working on a 12-inch circular needle, knit round 14 back onto the double-pointed needles; 24 sts per needle, 72 sts total remain)

Round 15: (k4, k2tog), repeat to end of round (20 sts per needle, 60 sts total remain)

Rounds 16 and 17: (k3, k2tog), repeat to end of round (16 sts per needle, 48 sts total remain)

Rounds 18–37: knit

Round 38: (k2, k2tog), repeat to end of round (12 sts per needle, 36 sts total remain)

Thread the tail from the cast-on end on a yarn needle, stitch through all the cast-on stitches, and gather to close the hole at the bottom. Stitch to secure. Fill the body one-third full with poly pellets and the rest with fiberfill, or stuff only with fiberfill.

Round 39: knit

Round 40: (k1, k2tog), repeat to end of round (8 sts per needle, 24 sts total remain)

Round 41: knit

Round 42: (k2tog), repeat to end of round (4 sts per needle, 12 sts total remain)

Finish stuffing firmly.

Round 43: (k1, k2tog, k1), repeat on each needle (3 sts per needle, 9 sts total remain)

Cut the yarn, leaving an 8-inch-long tail, and thread on a yarn needle. Pull through the remaining stitches, gather up tight to close the hole, and stitch to secure. Leave the end free to use later.

head

Starting at the back of the head with Daffodil and double-pointed needles, cast on 9 stitches, placing 3 stitches on each of three needles. Join to work in the round, being careful not to twist the stitches. Place a stitch marker on the first stitch.

Round 1: knit

Round 2: kfb in each stitch (6 sts per needle, 18 sts total)

Rounds 3 and 4: knit

Round 5: kfb in each stitch (12 sts per needle, 36 sts total)

Rounds 6–8: knit

Round 9: (k2, kfb), repeat to end of round (16 sts per needle, 48 sts total)

Round 10: knit

Round 11: (k3, kfb), repeat to end of round (20 sts per needle, 60 sts total)

Place a stitch marker on round 11 and leave it there. Knit every round until the head measures 2 inches from the stitch marker.

Decrease rounds

Round 1: (k3, k2tog), repeat to end of round (16 sts per needle, 48 sts total remain)

Round 2: knit

Round 3: (k2, k2tog), repeat to end of round (12 sts per needle, 36 sts total remain)

Rounds 4 and 5: knit

Place a stitch marker on round 5 and leave it there.

Round 6: (k1, ssk, k6, k2tog, k1), repeat on each needle (10 sts per needle, 30 sts total remain)

Knit every round until the nose measures 1 inch from the marker.

Decrease rounds for nose

Round 1: (k3, k2tog), repeat to end of round (8 sts per needle, 24 sts total remain)

Stuff with fiberfill.

Round 2: knit

Round 3: (k2, k2tog), repeat to end of round (6 sts per needle, 18 sts total remain)

Round 4: (k1, k2tog), repeat to end of round (4 sts per needle, 12 sts total remain)

Finish stuffing.

Round 5: (k1, k2tog, k1), repeat to end of round (3 sts per needle, 9 sts total remain)

Cut the yarn, leaving an 8-inch-long tail, and thread on a yarn needle. Pull through the remaining stitches, gather up tight to close the hole, and stitch to secure. Weave the tail to the inside and trim. Whipstitch the head to the body using a yarn needle and the tail from the neck.

legs (make 4)

With Daffodil and double-pointed needles, cast on 24 stitches, placing 8 stitches on each of three needles. Join to work in the round, being careful not to twist the stitches. Place a stitch marker on the first stitch.

Knit every round until the leg measures 6½ inches from the cast-on edge.

Switch to Orange and begin to work the hoof:

Round 1: (k1, m1, k6, m1, k1) on each needle
(10 sts per needle, 30 sts total)

Rounds 2–10: knit

Round 11: purl

Round 12: knit

Round 13: (k3, k2tog), repeat to end of round
(8 sts per needle, 24 sts total remain)

Round 14: (k2, k2tog), repeat to end of round
(6 sts per needle, 18 sts total remain)

Rounds 15 and 16: knit

Round 17: (k1, k2tog), repeat to end of round
(4 sts per needle, 12 sts total remain)

Round 18: (k1, k2tog, k1), repeat on each needle
(3 sts per needle, 9 sts total remain)

Cut the yarn, leaving an 8-inch-long tail, and thread on a yarn needle. Pull through the remaining stitches, gather up tight to close the hole, and stitch to secure. Weave the end to the inside and trim.

Fill the hooves with poly pellets and lightly stuff the legs with fiberfill, or stuff with fiberfill only. Whipstitch the top of the legs closed. Whipstitch two legs to the first decrease round on the body. Whipstitch two legs to the sides at the bottom of the body, using the photograph as a guide.

ears

outer ear (make 2)

With Daffodil and two double-pointed needles used as straight needles, cast on 10 stitches. Work in stockinette stitch (knit 1 row, purl 1 row) for 1 inch, ending with a purl row.

Increase rows

k1, m1, k to last stitch, m1, k1 (12 sts)

Next row: purl

Next row: repeat increase row (14 sts)

Continue in stockinette stitch until the ear measures 2 inches from the cast-on edge, ending with a purl row.

Decrease rows

Row 1: k1, ssk, k to last 3 sts, k2tog, k1
(12 sts remain)

Row 2: purl

Row 3: repeat row 1 (10 sts remain)

Row 4: p1, p2tog, p to the last 3 sts, p2tog, p1
(8 sts remain)

Row 5: k1, ssk, k2, k2tog, k1 (6 sts remain)

Row 6: p1, p2tog twice, p1 (4 sts remain)

Row 7: ssk, k2tog (2 sts remain)

Row 8: p2tog (1 st remains)

Cut the yarn, leaving an 8-inch-long tail and pull through the remaining stitch.

inner ear (make 2)

With Orange and two double-pointed needles used as straight needles, cast on 8 stitches. Work in stockinette stitch until the piece measures ¾ inch from the cast-on edge, ending with a purl row.

Increase rows

k1, m1, k to last st, m1, k1 (10 sts)

Next row: purl

Next row: increase row 1 (12 sts)

Continue in stockinette stitch until the piece measures 1¾ inches from the cast-on edge.

Decrease rows

Row 1: k1, ssk, k to last 3 sts, k2tog, k1
(10 sts remain)

Row 2: purl

Row 3: repeat row 1 (8 sts remain)

Row 4: p1, p2tog, p to the last 3 sts, p2tog, p1
(6 sts remain)

Row 5: k1, ssk, k2tog, k1 (4 sts remain)

Row 6: p2tog twice (2 sts remain)

Row 7: k2tog (1 st remains)

Cut the yarn and pull through the remaining stitch.

finishing

Place each inner ear piece on an outer ear piece, with purl sides facing and edges aligned. Whipstitch the inner and outer ears together along the edges, using the outer-ear tail threaded on a yarn needle. Pinch the cast-on edge together and whipstitch together ½ inch from the cast-on edge.

Whipstitch the ears to the side of the head, using the photograph as a guide.

tail

With Daffodil and double-pointed needles, cast on 9 stitches, placing 3 stitches on each of three needles. Join to knit in the round, being careful not to twist the stitches. Place a stitch marker on the first stitch.

Knit every round until the tail measures 2 inches from the cast-on edge. Cut the yarn, leaving a 6-inch-long tail, and thread on a yarn needle. Pull through the stitches, gather up tight to close, and stitch to secure. Stuff the tail lightly with fiberfill. Whipstitch the tail to the center lower back using the bound-off tail threaded on a yarn needle.

With Orange, make a 1-inch pom-pom with 30 wraps. Attach to the end of the tail with a yarn needle and the ends from the tie of the pom-pom.

horns (make 2)

With Daffodil and double-pointed needles, cast on 6 stitches, placing 2 stitches on each of three needles. Join to work in the round, being creful not to twist the stitches. Place a stitch marker on the first stitch. Knit every round until the horn measures 1 inch from the cast-on edge.

Next round: k2tog on each needle (3 sts total remain)

Cut the yarn, pull through the remaining stitches, and gather up tight to close. Weave the tail to the inside and trim. With Orange, make two 1-inch pom-poms with 30 wraps each. Attach to the tips of the horns with a yarn needle and the ends of the pom-pom ties.

Cut 2 pieces of a drinking straw ¾ inches long. Place the cut straw pieces inside the horns. Whipstitch the horns to the top of the head using a yarn needle and the tails from the cast-on end.

mane

With Orange, make eight 1-inch pom-poms with 30 wraps. Use the pom-pom tie ends and a yarn needle to attach the pom-poms, starting between the horns and continuing down the neck.

spots (make 11)

With Orange and two double-pointed needles used as straight needles, cast on 3 stitches.
Row 1: k1, m1, k1, m1, k1 (5 sts)
Row 2: purl
Row 3: k1, m1, k3, m1, k1 (7 sts)
Row 4: purl
Row 5: k1, m1, k5, m1, k1 (9 sts)
Row 6: purl
Row 7: knit
Row 8: purl
Row 9: ssk, k5, k2tog (7 sts)
Row 10: p2tog, p3, p2tog (5 sts)
Row 11: ssk, k1, k2tog (3 sts)

Bind off purlwise. Cut the yarn, leaving a 6-inch-long tail. Pull the tail through the remaining stitch.

When all of the spots are completed, pin them throughout the lower back and midback of the giraffe, using the photograph as a guide. Thread the tail from each dot on a yarn needle and whipstitch the dots in place.

face

With a yarn needle and a length of brown yarn, embroider the face using straight stitches (see p. 14) for the eyes and nose. Use the photograph on this book's cover as a guide.

4

sock-yarn toys

I know you have some sock yarn sitting around somewhere in your house, but in reality how many pairs of handknit socks can you own? My drawers are spilling over with them and it's too much already. I realized that I love the yarn but I needed to start finding some alternate projects to use it up. I've come to the conclusion that toys are the perfect project for sock yarn!

The good thing about the projects offered in this chapter is that you can substitute in any sock-weight yarn. Because most sock-weight yarn is about the same gauge, you can also combine your leftovers to make some fun stripey toys, too. Included are some fruits to put on your fingers, a sweet bear, a lanky-armed monkey, a round little hippo, and a curlicue snake. So grab a ball of your favorite sock yarn and get busy knitting up your favorite sock-yarn toy!

finger foods

When I got these beautiful mini-skeins of sock yarn, I was inspired. Even though I'd had something else in mind for the yarn, the small size of the skeins and the gorgeous colors made me think of nothing but fruit.

As a twist, I made the fruit into finger puppets. Each piece of fruit has a hole knit into the underside so it can be placed on a little finger, on a bedpost, or even on top of a knitting needle sitting in a jar.

Whether you knit up a Pear, Apple, or Bunch of Grapes, these speedy projects will take a juicy bite out of your sock yarn stash.

finished measurements
- 3½ inches tall

yarn
- Sunshine Yarns Soft Superwash mini-skeins (100% merino wool; 60–70 yards), 1 skein each in Buttermilk, Lime, Sunshine, Avocado, Fire Orange, Chocolate, and Dusty Plum

NOTE • Any fingering-weight sock yarn will work for this project.

tools
- U.S. size 3 set of four double-pointed needles, or size needed to obtain gauge
- Scissors
- Tape measure or ruler
- Stitch markers
- Yarn needle
- Polyester fiberfill, 1 small bag

gauge
- 6 stitches per inch in stockinette stitch

pear
finger
With Buttermilk, cast on 9 stitches, placing 3 stitches on each of three double-pointed needles. Join to knit in the round, being careful not to twist the stitches. Place a stitch marker on the first stitch.

Round 1: knit

Round 2: kfb in each stitch (6 sts per needle, 18 sts total)

Round 3: knit

Round 4: (k1, kfb), repeat across the round (9 sts per needle, 27 sts total)

Knit every round until the finger measures 2 inches from the cast on.

Continue on to create the body of the Pear:
Switch to Lime or Sunshine.

Rounds 1 and 2: knit

Round 3: (k2, m1) 4 times, k1 on each needle (13 sts per needle, 39 sts total)

Rounds 4 and 5: knit

Round 6: (k3, m1) 4 times, k1 on each needle (17 sts per needle, 51 sts total)

Round 7: knit

Round 8: (k2, m1, k7, m1, k6, m1, k2) on each needle (20 sts per needle, 60 sts total)

Place a stitch marker on round 8 and leave it there. Knit every round until the Pear measures 1¼ inches from the marker.

Decrease rounds

Round 1: (k3, k2tog), repeat across the round (16 sts per needle, 48 sts total remain)

Rounds 2 and 3: knit

Round 4: (k2, k2tog), repeat across the round (12 sts per needle, 36 sts total remain)

Rounds 5–12: knit

Round 13: (k2, k2tog), repeat across the round (9 sts per needle, 27 sts total remain)

Rounds 14 and 15: knit

Push the finger so that it goes up into the inside of the Pear. Stuff the Pear with fiberfill around the finger. Continue to stuff as you work to the end.

Round 16: (k1, k2tog), repeat across the round (6 sts per needle, 18 sts total remain)

Round 17: knit

Round 18: (k1, k2tog), repeat across the round (4 sts per needle, 12 sts total remain)

Round 19: (k1, k2tog, k1), repeat on each needle (3 sts per needle, 9 sts total remain)

Finish stuffing the Pear.

Round 20: (k1, k2tog), repeat on each needle (2 sts per needle, 6 sts total remain)

Continue on to create the stem:

Switch to Buttermilk. Knit all 6 stitches onto 1 double-pointed needle.

Working on two needles in I-cord (see p. 7), k2tog across the row, leaving 3 stitches remaining. Continue in I-cord until the stem measures 1 inch. Bind off. Cut the yarn, leaving a 6-inch-long tail, and pull through the remaining stitch. Thread the tail on a yarn needle and weave through the I-cord and into the Pear.

(see p. 7)

leaf

With Avocado and two double-pointed needles used as straight needles, cast on 5 stitches, leaving a 4-inch-long tail.

Row 1: k2, yo, k2tog, k1 (5 sts)

Row 2: purl

Rows 3 and 4: repeat rows 1 and 2

Row 5: ssk, yo, k2tog, k1 (4 sts remain)

Row 6: p2tog twice, pass the second stitch over the first stitch (1 st remains)

Cut the yarn and pull through the remaining stitch. Weave the end into the back of the leaf. Thread the tail from the cast-on edge on a yarn needle. Stitch through all of the cast-on stitches, pull up the cast-on edge to close the hole, and stitch to secure. Whipstitch the leaf to the bottom of the stem. Weave the end to the inside of the Pear and trim.

apple

finger

Cast on with Chocolate and work the same as for the Pear.

Continue on to create the body of the Apple:

Change to Fire Orange and work rounds 1–8 as for the pear. Place a stitch marker on round 8 and leave it there. Knit every round until the Apple measures 2½ inches from the marker.

Decrease rounds

Round 1: (k3, k2tog), repeat across the round (16 sts per needle, 48 sts total remain)

Rounds 2 and 3: knit

Round 4: (k2, k2tog), repeat across the round (12 sts per needle, 36 sts total remain)

Round 5: knit

Turn the finger up into the Apple. Stuff the Apple with fiberfill.

Round 6: (k2, k2tog), repeat across the round (9 sts per needle, 27 sts total remain)

Round 7: knit

Round 8: (k1, k2tog), repeat across the round (6 sts per needle, 18 sts total remain)

Round 9: k2tog, repeat across the round (3 sts per needle, 9 sts total remain)

Finish stuffing the Apple.

Continue on to create the stem:

Switch to Chocolate.

Next round: k2tog, repeat across the round, knit the last stitch (5 sts remain)

Place all of the stitches on one needle.

Using two double-pointed needles, work in I-cord to complete the stem as follows:

Row 1: k2tog, k3 (4 sts remain)

Row 2: k2tog, k2 (3 sts remain)

Work in I-cord until the stem measures 1 inch. Bind off.

Finish as for the Pear. Add a leaf in Avocado, as for the Pear.

bunch of grapes

finger

Cast on with Avocado and complete the same as for the pear finger.

Bind off. Cut the yarn and pull through the remaining stitches.

grapes

large grape (make 10)

With Dusty Plum cast on 9 stitches and place 3 stitches on each of three double-pointed needles. Join to work in the round, being careful not to twist the stitches. Place a marker on the first stitch.

Round 1: knit

Round 2: kfb in each stitch (6 sts per needle, 18 sts total)

Rounds 3 and 4: knit

Round 5: (kfb, k4, kfb) on each needle (8 sts per needle, 24 sts total)

Rounds 6–9: knit

Round 10: (k2tog, k4, k2tog) on each needle (6 sts per needle, 18 sts total remain)

With a yarn needle and the tail from the cast-on edge, stitch through all of the cast-on stitches, gather to close the hole at the bottom, and stitch to secure (see p. 76). Weave the tail inside of the Grape. Stuff the Grape with fiberfill.

Rounds 11 and 12: knit

Round 13: k2tog, repeat across the round (3 sts per needle, 9 sts total remain)

Round 14: knit.

Finish stuffing. Cut the yarn, leaving a 6-inch-long tail, and thread on a yarn needle. Pull the tail through the remaining stitches, gather up tight to close the hole, and stitch to secure. Leave the tail free to sew the Grapes to the finger later.

small grape (make 6)

Rounds 1 and 2: work as for the large Grape

Rounds 3–6: knit

Close and stuff as for the large Grape.

Round 7: (k2tog), repeat across the round (3 sts per needle, 9 sts total remain)

Round 8: knit

Complete as for the large Grape.

finishing

With the tails and a yarn needle, sew the grapes to the finger. Arrange the large Grapes and attach first by taking a few stitches through the Grape and the finger. Then fill in any spaces with the small Grapes to make it look like a bunch.

vines

With Avocado and two double-pointed needles used as straight needles, cast on 20 stitches.

Bind off 19 stitches, tightly, leaving 1 stitch on the needle.

Cast on 19 stitches using the backward-loop method. (20 stitches).

Repeat this 4 more times until you have 5 squiggly vines total.

Weave in the tail and sew the vines to the top of the Bunch of Grapes.

baby bear

Every toy collection needs a bear or two, right? Knitting this simple small bear is the perfect way to use up some leftover sock yarn. When I decided to make Baby Bear, I looked straight to my Noro sock yarn in my favorite Kureyon colorway. You may recognize it from the Inca Snowflake hat in *Itty-Bitty Hats*. I just can't get enough!

You can use a solid, semisolid, or self-striping yarn to create this bear. Utterly sweet, with minimal seaming, this is an easy toy to make and love.

finished measurements
- 7½ inches tall when seated, 4 inches wide

yarn
- Kureyon Sock yarn (70% wool, 30% nylon; 420 meters/100 grams), 1 skein in Colorway S95

NOTE • Any fingering-weight sock yarn will work for this project.

tools
- U.S. size 3 set of four double-pointed needles, or size needed to obtain gauge
- Stitch markers
- Tape measure or ruler
- Scissors
- Yarn needle
- Polyester fiberfill, 1 small bag
- Poly pellets (optional), 32-ounce bag
- Black embroidery floss
- Embroidery needle

gauge
- 6½ stitches per inch in stockinette stitch

body

Cast on 9 stitches, placing 3 stitches on each of three double-pointed needles. Join to work in the round, being careful not to twist the stitches. Place a stitch marker on the first stitch.

Increase rounds
Round 1 and every odd round: knit
Round 2: kfb in each stitch (6 sts per needle, 18 sts total)
Round 4: (k1, kfb), repeat across the round (9 sts per needle, 27 sts total)
Round 6: (k2, kfb), repeat across the round (12 sts per needle, 36 sts total)
Round 8: (k3, kfb), repeat across the round (15 sts per needle, 45 sts total)
Round 10: (k4, kfb), repeat across the round (18 sts per needle, 54 sts total)
Round 12: (k5, kfb), repeat across the round (21 sts per needle, 63 sts total)
Round 14: (k6, kfb), repeat across the round (24 sts per needle, 72 sts total)
Round 16: (k7, kfb), repeat across the round (27 sts per needle, 81 sts total)

Place a stitch marker on round 16 and leave it there.

Knit every round until the body measures 2½ inches from the stitch marker.

Decrease rounds
Round 1: (k7, k2tog), repeat across the round (24 sts per needle, 72 sts total remain)
Rounds 2–7: knit
Round 8: (k6, k2tog), repeat across the round (21 sts per needle, 63 sts total remain)

Rounds 9–12: knit

Round 13: (k5, k2tog), repeat across the round (18 sts per needle, 54 sts total remain)

Round 14: (k4, k2tog), repeat across the round (15 sts per needle, 45 sts total remain)

Round 15: knit

Thread the end from the cast-on stitches on a yarn needle and stitch through all of the cast-on stitches. Gather up to close the hole at the bottom of the body and stitch to secure. Fill the bottom of the body about one-third full with poly pellets or use only the fiberfill. Continue to add stuffing as you finish the top of the body.

Round 16: (k3, k2tog), repeat across the round (12 sts per needle, 36 sts total remain)

Round 17: knit

Round 18: (k2, k2tog), repeat across the round (9 sts per needle, 27 sts total remain)

Round 19: knit

Round 20: (k1, k2tog), repeat across the round (6 sts per needle, 18 sts total remain)

Round 21: k2tog, repeat across the round (3 sts per needle, 9 sts total remain)

Finish stuffing the body. Cut the yarn, leaving an 8-inch-long tail. Thread the tail on a yarn needle, pull through the remaining stitches, and gather up tight to close the hole, leaving the tail out for later use.

head

Starting at the back of the head, work the same as for the body through round 12 (21 sts per needle, 63 sts total). Place a stitch marker on round 12 and leave it there.

Knit every round until the head measures 2 inches from the marker.

Continue on to create the face and nose:

Round 1: (k5, k2tog), repeat across the round (18 sts per needle, 54 sts total remain)

Round 2: (k4, k2tog), repeat across the round (15 sts per needle, 45 sts total remain)

Rounds 3 and 4: knit

Thread the end from the cast-on stitches on a yarn needle, stitch through all cast-on stitches, and gather to close the hole. Stitch to secure.

Weave the end to the inside and trim. Stuff the head with fiberfill and continue to add stuffing as you work.

Round 5: (k3, k2tog), repeat across the round (12 sts per needle, 36 sts total remain)

Round 6: (k2, k2tog), repeat across the round (9 sts per needle, 27 sts total remain)

Rounds 7–11: knit

Round 12: (k1, k2tog), repeat across the round (6 sts per needle, 18 sts total remain)

Round 13: knit

Round 14: k2tog, repeat across the round (3 sts per needle, 9 sts total remain)

Complete stuffing the head. Cut the yarn, leaving a 6-inch-long tail, and thread the tail on a yarn needle. Pull the end through the remaining stitches, gather up tight to close the hole, and stitch to secure. Weave the end to the inside and trim. Place the tail from the top of the body on a yarn needle, and whipstitch the head to the top of the body.

arms (make 2)

Cast on 21 stitches, placing 7 stitches on each of three double-pointed needles. Join to work in the round, being careful not to twist the stitches. Place a stitch marker on the first stitch.

Knit every round until the arm measures 2 inches from the cast-on round.

Continue on to create the wrist and hand:

Round 1: (k5, k2tog), repeat on each needle (6 sts per needle, 18 sts total remain)

Round 2: (k4, k2tog), repeat on each needle (5 sts per needle, 15 sts total remain)

Round 3: knit

Round 4: (k4, m1, k1), repeat on each needle (6 sts per needle, 18 sts total)

Round 5: (k5, m1, k1), repeat on each needle (7 sts per needle, 21 sts total)

Round 6: (k6, m1, k1), repeat on each needle (8 sts per needle, 24 sts total)

Rounds 7–14: knit

Round 15: (k2, k2tog), repeat across the round (6 sts per needle, 18 sts total remain)

Round 16: knit

Round 17: (k1, k2tog), repeat across the round (4 sts per needle, 12 sts total remain)

Round 18: knit

Round 19: (k1, k2tog, k1), repeat on each needle (3 sts per needle, 9 sts total remain)

Cut the yarn and thread the tail on a yarn needle. Pull through the remaining stitches, gather up tight to close the hole, and stitch to secure. Weave the end to the inside and trim.

Stuff the arm by either filling the hand with poly pellets and filling the rest of the arm with fiberfill, or use only the fiberfill. Thread the end from the cast-on stitches on a yarn needle and whipstitch the top of the arm closed. Whipstitch the arms to the sides of the body, using the photograph as a guide.

legs (make 2)

Begin the same as for the arms. Knit until leg measure 2½ inches from the cast-on edge. Bind off.

Cut the yarn and pull through the last stitch, leaving a 6-inch-long tail.

feet (make 2)

Cast on 9 stitches, placing 3 stitches on each of three double-pointed needles. Join to work in the round, being careful not to twist the stitches. Place a stitch marker on the first stitch.

Round 1: knit

Round 2: kfb in each stitch (6 sts per needle, 18 sts total)

Round 3: knit

Round 4: (k1, kfb), repeat across the round (9 sts per needle, 27 sts total)

Knit every round until the foot measures 1¼ inches from the cast-on edge.

Next round: (k1, k2tog), repeat across the round (6 sts per needle, 18 sts total remain)

Stuff the foot with poly pellets or polyfill.

Divide the remaining stitches, placing 9 stitches on each of two needles.

Next round: (ssk, k5, k2tog) on each needle (7 sts per needle, 14 sts total remain)

Cut the yarn, leaving an 8-inch-long tail, and thread on a yarn needle. Use kitchener stitch (see p. 9) to graft the toe of the foot closed.

Whipstitch the feet to the bottom of the legs, using the tails from the cast-on edges. Stuff the legs with fiberfill and whipstitch to the front of the body, using the photograph as a guide.

ears (make 2)

Cast on 18 stitches, placing 6 stitches on each of three double-pointed needles.

Rounds 1–3: knit

Round 4: (k1, k2tog), repeat across the round (4 sts per needle, 12 sts total remain)

Round 5: (k2, k2tog) on each needle (3 sts per needle, 9 sts total remain)

Cut the yarn, leaving a 6-inch tail, and thread the tail on a yarn needle. Pull through the remaining stitches, gather up tight to close the hole, and stitch to secure. Weave the end to the inside and trim.

Thread the end of the tail from the cast-on stitches on a yarn needle. Fold each ear flat widthwise and whipstitch the two sides of the cast-on edge together. Whipstitch the ears to the head, using the photograph as a guide.

tail

Cast on 12 stitches, placing 4 stitches on each of three double-pointed needles. Join to work in the round, being careful not to twist the stitches. Place a marker on the first stitch.

Rounds 1–3: knit

Round 4: (k2, k2tog), repeat on each needle (3 sts per needle, 9 sts total remain)

Cut the yarn, leaving a 6-inch-long tail, and thread on a yarn needle. Pull through the remaining stitches, gather up tight to close the hole, and stitch to secure. Weave the end to the inside and trim. Stuff the tail lightly, then thread the cast-on tail on a yarn needle, and use it to whipstitch the tail to the lower back of the body.

eyes, nose, and mouth

Using the embroidery floss and the embroidery needle, create the eyes with the spiderweb technique (see p. 13). Create a triangle-shaped nose using satin stitch (see p. 14) and a mouth using straight stitches (see p. 14), using the photograph as a guide.

a new sock monkey

Because I adore the old-fashioned sock monkeys made with real socks that are cut up and pieced together, I had to include my own version here.

This little guy is one of my favorite toys of the entire collection. He turned out with a personality that makes me smile. Maybe it's the hair? His long, dangly arms and his melancholy expression add to his sweetness.

Use some of your self-striping sock yarn or just a single color; either way, you are going to want to make one for everyone you know.

finished measurements

- 5 inches tall when seated, 4 inches wide

yarn

- Yarntini Hand Dyed Yarns Sock Stripe (100% merino wool; 430 yards), 1 skein in Chocolatini

---

NOTE • Any fingering-weight sock yarn will work for this project.

---

tools

- U.S. size 3 set of four double-pointed needles, or size needed to obtain gauge
- Tape measure or ruler
- Yarn needle
- Scissors
- Stitch markers
- Polyester fiberfill, 1 small bag
- Poly pellets (optional), 32-ounce bag
- Black embroidery floss

gauge

- 7 stitches per inch in stockinette stitch

body

Cast on 9 stitches, placing 3 stitches on each of three double-pointed needles. Join to work in the round, being careful not to twist the stitches. Place a stitch marker on the first stitch.

Round 1: knit

Round 2: kfb in each stitch (6 sts per needle, 18 sts total)

Round 3: knit

Round 4: kfb in each stitch (12 sts per needle, 36 sts total)

Rounds 5–7: knit

Round 8: (k2, kfb), repeat across the round (16 sts per needle, 48 sts total)

Round 9: knit

Round 10: (k3, kfb), repeat across the round (20 sts per needle, 60 sts total)

Place a stitch marker on round 10 and leave it there. Knit every round until the body measures 3 inches from the stitch marker.

Decrease rounds

Round 1: (k3, k2tog), repeat across the round (16 sts per needle, 48 sts total remain)

Rounds 2–5: knit

Round 6: (k2, k2tog), repeat across the round (12 sts per needle, 36 sts total remain)

Rounds 7–10: knit

Thread the tail from the cast-on stitches on a yarn needle. Stitch through all of the cast-on stitches, pull up tight to gather, and stitch to secure. Stuff the body one-third full with poly pellets and the rest with fiberfill, or with fiberfill only.

Round 11: (k1, k2tog), repeat across the round (8 sts per needle, 24 sts total remain)

Round 12: knit

Round 13: k2tog, repeat across the round (4 sts per needle, 12 sts total remain)

Round 14: (k2tog, k2), repeat across the round (3 sts per needle, 9 sts total remain)

Finish stuffing the body. Cut the yarn, leaving a 6-inch-long tail, and thread the tail on a yarn needle. Pull the end through the remaining stitches, gather up tight to close the hole, and stitch to secure.

head

Starting at the bottom of the head, work the same as for the body through round 8 (16 sts per needle, 48 sts total).

Rounds 9–20: knit

Round 21: (k2, k2tog), repeat across the round (12 sts per needle, 36 sts total remain)

Rounds 22 and 23: knit

Round 24: (k1, k2tog), repeat across the round (8 sts per needle, 24 sts total remain)

Thread the tail from the cast-on stitches on a yarn needle. Stitch through all of the cast-on stitches, pull up to close the hole, and stitch to secure. Stuff the head with fiberfill.

Round 25: knit

Round 26: k2tog, repeat across the round (4 sts per needle, 12 sts total remain)

Round 27: knit

Cut the yarn, leaving an 8-inch-long tail, and thread on a yarn needle. Pull the end through the remaining stitches, gather up tight to close the hole, and stitch to secure. Leave the remaining tail free.

nose

Cast on 27 stitches, placing 9 stitches on each of three double-pointed needles. Join to work in the round, being careful not to twist the stitches. Place a stitch marker on the first stitch.

Rounds 1–4: knit

Round 5: (k1, k2tog), repeat across the round (6 sts per needle, 18 sts total remain)

Round 6: knit

Round 7: k2tog, repeat across the round (3 sts per needle, 9 sts total remain)

Cut the yarn, leaving an 8-inch-long tail, and thread the end on a yarn needle. Pull the end through the remaining stitches, pull up tight to close the hole, and stitch to secure. Weave the tail to the inside and trim. Stuff the nose lightly and thread the tail from the cast-on stitches on a yarn needle. Whipstitch the nose to the head, weave the tail to the inside, and trim.

Whipstitch the head to the body using the remaining bound-off tail.

ears (make 2)

Cast on 12 stitches, placing 4 stitches on each of three double-pointed needles. Join to work in the round, being careful not to twist the stitches. Place a stitch marker on the first stitch.

Rounds 1–4: knit

Round 5: (k2, k2tog), repeat across the round (3 sts per needle, 9 sts total remain)

Cut the yarn and thread the tail on a yarn needle. Pull the tail through the remaining stitches, gather up tight to close the hole, and stitch to secure. Weave the tail to the inside and trim.

Thread the tail from the cast-on stitches on a yarn needle. Whipstitch the cast-on edge of each ear together so the ear lays flat. Whipstitch the ears to the head, using the photograph as a guide. Weave the tail to the inside and trim.

arms (make 2)

Cast on 9 stitches, placing 3 stitches on each of three double-pointed needles. Join to work in the round, being careful not to twist the stitches. Place a stitch marker on the first stitch.

Knit every round until the arm measures 3½ inches from the cast-on edge.

Continue on to create the hand:

Round 1: (k1, m1, k2), repeat on each needle (12 sts total)

Round 2: k5, m1, k2, m1, k5 (14 sts total)

Round 3: knit

Round 4:

Needle 1: k1, m1, k3 (5 sts)

Needle 2: k1, m1, k3, m1, k2 (8 sts)

Needle 3: k3, m1, k1 (5 sts, 18 sts total)

Round 5:

Needle 1: knit (6 sts)

Needle 2: knit (6 sts)

Needle 3: knit (6 sts)

Round 6:

Needle 1: knit

Needle 2: skip over and go to needle 3

Needle 3: knit

Rounds 7–11: Knit every stitch only on needles 1 and 3 (12 sts). Leave needle 2 alone.

Round 12: (k1, k2tog), repeat across needles 1 and 3 (4 sts per needle, 8 sts total remain)

Round 13: (k2tog), repeat across needles 1 and 3 (2 sts per needle, 4 sts total remain)

Fill the hand with poly pellets or fiberfill.

Cut the yarn, leaving a 6-inch-long tail, and thread on a yarn needle. Pull through the remaining stitches, gather up tight to close the hole, and stitch to secure.

thumb

Reattach the yarn to knit on the stitches remaining on needle 2. Place 2 stitches on each of three double-pointed needles.

Rounds 1–3: knit

Cut the yarn and thread on a yarn needle. Pull through the remaining stitches, gather up tight, and stitch to secure. Weave through to the inside of the hand and trim.

Whipstitch the arms to the sides of the body, using the arm cast-on tails. Weave tails to the inside and trim.

legs (make 2)

Work the same as for the arms, but only knit until the leg measures 3 inches from the cast-on edge.

To make the feet bend upward, take a few stitches to connect the top of the foot to the leg. Whipstitch the legs to the body, using the cast-on tails. Weave the tails to the inside and trim.

hair

With two double-pointed needles used as straight needles, cast on 10 stitches.

Row 1: work a twisted loop stitch in every stitch as follows:

Knit the stitch and leave it on the left needle.

Pull the loop that is on the right needle out about 1 inch. Transfer the loop onto your right index finger. Twist the loop in one direction until it folds back on itself.

Place the loop back on the left needle.

Knit the two stitches together.

Row 2: knit

Row 3: repeat row 1

Bind off by knitting 2 stitches together at a time. Cut the yarn, leaving a 6-inch-long tail, and thread on a yarn needle. Pull through the remaining stitch. Whipstitch the hair to the top of the head, using the photograph as a guide. Weave the end to the inside and trim.

face

With black embroidery floss and a yarn needle, make the eyes, nose, and mouth with straight stitches (see p. 14), using the photograph as a guide.

hippo

In the wild, hippos may not be cute and friendly, but this one is! For this adorable round little friend I held two strands of sock yarn together throughout and still had a lot of yarn left at the end. The doubled yarn gives the hippo a substantial feel when finished. The pattern is simple, with minimal seaming and fewer pieces, and you can complete it in a shorter amount of time because of the larger needle size and doubled yarn. This one is just right all-around!

finished measurements
- 7 inches tall when seated, 4½ inches wide

yarn
- Dream in Color Smooshy Sock Yarn (100% superfine Australian superwash merino; 450 yards/4 ounces.), 1 skein in Wisterious VS240
- Koigu KPM (100% merino wool; 175 yards/ 50 grams), 1 skein in Light Pink #2232 (Optional; just a small amount is needed for the foot pads and inner ears. The entire hippo could be done in one color.)

tools
- U.S. size 5 set of four double-pointed needles, or size needed to obtain gauge
- Tape measure or ruler
- Polyester fiberfill, 1 small bag
- Poly pellets (optional), 32-ounce bag
- Scissors
- Yarn needle
- Black embroidery floss
- Stitch markers

gauge
- 6 stitches per inch in stockinette stitch with two strands held together

TIP • Wind the skein in a center-pull ball, then pull from the inside and outside of the ball. Or wind two separate balls to pull the strands from.

body
With two strands of Wisterious held together, cast on 9 stitches, placing 3 stitches on each of three double-pointed needles. Join to work in the round, being careful not to twist the stitches. Place a stitch marker on the first stitch.

Round 1: knit

Round 2: kfb in each stitch (6 sts per needle, 18 sts total)

Rounds 3 and 4: knit

Round 5: (k2, kfb), repeat across the round (8 sts per needle, 24 sts total)

Round 6: knit

Round 7: (k1, kfb), repeat across the round (12 sts per needle, 36 sts total)

Rounds 8 and 9: knit

Round 10: (k1, kfb), repeat across the round (18 sts per needle, 54 sts total)

Round 11: (kfb, knit to last st, kfb), repeat on each needle (20 sts per needle, 60 sts total)

Rounds 12–14: knit

Round 15: (k3, kfb), repeat across the round (25 sts per needle, 75 sts total)

Place a stitch marker on round 15 and leave it there. Knit every round until the body measures 4 inches from the stitch marker.

Decrease rounds
Round 1: (k3, k2tog), repeat across the round (20 sts per needle, 60 sts total remain)

Round 2: knit

Round 3: (k2, k2tog), repeat across the round (15 sts per needle, 45 sts total remain)

Rounds 4 and 5: knit

Round 6: (k1, k2tog), repeat across the round (10 sts per needle, 30 sts total remain)

Rounds 7 and 8: knit

Thread the tail from the cast-on stitches on a yarn needle. Stitch through all of the cast-on stitches, pull up tight to close the hole, and stitch to secure. Weave the end to the inside and trim.

Begin to stuff the body with one-third poly pellets and the rest with fiberfill, or with fiberfill only.

Round 9: (k3, k2tog), repeat across the round (8 sts per needle, 24 sts total remain)

Round 10: (k2, k2tog), repeat across the round (6 sts per needle, 18 sts total remain)

Round 11: (k1, k2tog), repeat across the round (4 sts per needle, 12 sts total remain)

Round 12: (k1, k2tog, k1), repeat across the round (3 sts per needle, 9 sts total remain)

Finish stuffing the body with fiberfill.

Cut the yarn, leaving an 8-inch-long tail, and thread the tail on a yarn needle. Pull the end through the remaining stitches, gather up tight to close the hole, and stitch to secure. Leave the tail free for use later.

head

Work the same as for the body through round 10 (18 sts per needle, 54 sts total).

Place a stitch marker on round 10 and leave it there. Knit every round until the head measures 2 inches from the marker.

Decrease rounds

Round 1: (k4, k2tog), repeat across the round (15 sts per needle, 45 sts total remain)

Round 2: (k3, k2tog), repeat across the round (12 sts per needle, 36 sts total remain)

Round 3: (k2, k2tog), repeat across the round (9 sts per needle, 27 sts total remain)

Continue on to create the nose:

Round 1: (k3, m1), repeat across the round (12 sts per needle, 36 sts total)

Rounds 2–5: knit

Round 6: (k4, m1), repeat across the round (15 sts per needle, 45 sts total)

Rounds 7–12: knit

Round 13: (k3, k2tog), repeat across the round (12 sts per needle, 36 sts total remain)

Round 14: (k2, k2tog), repeat across the round (9 sts per needle, 27 sts total remain)

Rounds 15 and 16: knit

Round 17: (k1, k2tog), repeat across the round (6 sts per needle, 18 sts total remain)

Stuff the head with fiberfill.

Divide the stitches, placing 9 stitches on each of two double-pointed needles so that the 9 stitches making up the upper lip are on one needle, and those for the lower lip are on the other. Cut the yarn, leaving a 12-inch-long tail, and thread on a yarn needle. Use kitchener stitch (see p. 9) to graft the nose closed. Weave the end to the inside and trim.

With the bound-off tail from the body threaded on a yarn needle, whipstitch the head to the top of the body.

arms (make 2)

With two strands of Wisterious held together, cast on 18 stitches, placing 6 stitches on each of three double-pointed needles. Join to work in the round, being careful not twist the stitches. Place a stitch marker on the first stitch.

Knit every round until the arm measures 2 inches from the cast-on edge.

Continue on to create the hand:

Round 1:

Needle 1: knit (6 sts)

Needles 2 and 3: (k2, m1), repeat to end of round (9 sts, 24 sts total)

Round 2:

Needle 1: (k1, k2tog) 2 times (4 sts remain)

Needles 2 and 3: (k3, m1) 6 times (12 sts per needle, 28 sts total)

Rounds 3–6: knit

Switch to Light Pink or continue with Wisterious.

Round 7:

Needle 1: knit (4 sts)

Needles 2 and 3: (k2, k2tog) 6 times
(9 sts per needle remain)
  22 stitches total remain.
Round 8: knit
Round 9:
Needle 1: knit (4 sts)
Needles 2 and 3: (k1, k2tog) 6 times
(6 sts per needle, 16 sts total remain)
Round 10:
Needle 1: knit (4 sts)
Needles 2 and 3: (k1, k2tog) 4 times
(4 sts per needle remain)
  12 sts total remain
Round 11: (k1, k2tog, k1) on each needle
(3 sts per needle, 9 sts total remain)
  Cut the yarn, threading the tail on a yarn needle. Pull the end through the remaining stitches, gather up tight to close the hole, and stitch to secure. Weave the end to the inside and trim.

Stuff the hands with poly pellets and the arms with fiberfill, or stuff with fiberfill only. Thread a length of yarn on a yarn needle and use a running stitch (see p. 14) to create definition in the wrists. Gather loosely and tie the ends to secure. Weave the ends to the inside and trim. Whipstitch the top of each arm closed with the cast-on tail threaded on a yarn needle. Whipstitch the arms to the sides of the body, using the photograph as a guide.

legs (make 2)

With two strands of Wisterious held together, cast on 24 stitches and place 8 stitches on each of three double-pointed needles. Join to work in the round, being careful not to twist the stitches. Place a stitch marker on the first stitch.

  Knit every round until the leg measures 2½ inches from the cast-on edge.

Continue on to create the foot:
Round 1:
Needle 1: knit (8 sts)
Needles 2 and 3: k1 (m1, k2) 3 times, m1, k1 on each needle (12 sts per needle)
  32 stitches total.
Round 2:
Needle 1: (k2, k2tog) 2 times (6 sts remain)
Needles 2 and 3: (k3, m1) 4 times on each needle (16 sts per needle)
  38 stitches total.
Rounds 3–8: knit
  Switch to Light Pink or just continue on with Wisterious.
Round 9:
Needle 1: knit (6 sts)
Needles 2 and 3: (k2, k2tog) 4 times on each needle (12 sts per needle remain)
  30 stitches total remain.
Round 10: knit

Round 11:
Needle 1: knit (6 sts)
Needles 2 and 3: (k2, k2tog) 3 times on each needle (9 sts per needle remain)
 24 stitches total remain.
Rounds 12 and 13: knit
Round 14:
Needle 1: knit (6 sts)
Needles 2 and 3: (k1, k2tog) 3 times on each needle (6 sts per needle remain)
 18 stitches total remain.
Round 15: (k1, k2tog), repeat across the round (4 sts per needle, 12 sts total remain)
Round 16: (k1, k2tog, k1), repeat on each needle (3 sts per needle, 9 sts total remain)

Cut the yarn, leaving a 6-inch-long tail, and thread the tail on a yarn needle. Pull through the remaining stitches, gather up tight to close the hole, and stitch to secure. Weave the end to the inside and trim.

Stuff the feet with poly pellets and the legs with fiberfill, or both with fiberfill only. With a length of yarn threaded on a yarn needle, gather loosely, using a running stitch as for the wrists. Tie to secure, weave the ends to the inside, and trim.

Whipstitch the top of each leg closed with the cast-on tail threaded on a yarn needle. Whipstitch the legs to the body, using the photograph as a guide.

ears
outer ear (make 2)
With two strands of Wisterious held together and two double-pointed needles used as straight needles, cast on 9 stitches.
Row 1: knit
Row 2: purl
Rows 3 and 4: repeat rows 1 and 2
Row 5: k1, ssk, k3, k2tog, k1 (7 sts remain)
Row 6: p1, p2tog, p1, p2tog, p1 (5 sts remain)
 Bind off. Cut the yarn, leaving a 6-inch-long tail, and pull through the remaining stitch.

inner ear (make 2)
With two strands of either Wisterious or Light Pink held together and two double-pointed needles used as straight needles, cast on 7 stitches.

Rows 1–4: work the same as for the outer ear
Row 5: k1, ssk, k1, k2tog, k1 (5 sts remain)
Row 6: p1, p2tog, p2tog (3 sts remain)
 Bind off. Cut the yarn, leaving a 6-inch-long tail, and pull through the remaining stitch.

finishing
Place one outer ear piece on each inner ear piece, purl sides facing, and whipstitch the edges together using the tails from the outer ears threaded on a yarn needle. Fold in the outer edges at the base of the ear and stitch together to secure. Whipstitch the ears to the head, using the photograph as a guide. Weave all ends to the inside and trim.

tail
With two strands of Wisterious held together, cast on 12 stitches, placing 4 stitches on each of three double-pointed needles. Join to work in the round, being careful not to twist the stitches. Place a stitch marker on the first stitch.

Knit every round until the tail measures 1 inch from the cast-on edge.

Decrease rounds
Round 1: (k2, k2tog) on each needle (3 sts per needle, 9 sts total remain)
Rounds 2 and 3: knit
Round 4: (k1, k2tog) on each needle (2 sts per needle, 6 sts total remain)

Cut the yarn, leaving a 6-inch-long tail, and thread on a yarn needle. Pull through the remaining stitches, gather up tight to close the hole, and stitch to secure. Weave the end to the inside and trim. Stuff the tail lightly with fiberfill through the cast-on end. Whipstitch the tail to the lower back of the body with the cast-on tail threaded on a yarn needle, weave in ends, and trim.

face
With the black embroidery floss threaded on a yarn needle, take two small straight stitches (see p. 14) for the eyes, using the photograph as a guide. To create the mouth, make one long straight stitch and secure it with a couple of small stitches to hold it in place.

curly snake

This curly snake is perfect to wrap around your shoulders, the arm of a chair, or a crib rail. He is welcome to hang out just about anywhere. The entire snake is knit in one piece in the round; you just knit and knit and knit. Not only is it fast, it's so simple you could make this curly friend in your sleep.

Starting at the tail, you knit the snake until he is as long as you like, using up any stash of sock yarn and leftovers along the way. A simple running stitch along the side, when pulled, makes the snake curl up.

finished measurements

- 24 inches long when uncurled

yarn

- Trekking (XXL) (75% new wool, 25% nylon; 459 yards/100 grams), Circus#135

NOTE • Any fingering-weight sock yarn will work for this project, and it takes only a small portion of a skein. Leftover, odd balls will be sufficient.

tools

- U.S. size 3 set of four double-pointed needles, or size needed to obtain gauge
- Scissors
- Tape measure or ruler
- Polyester fiberfill, 1 small bag
- Yarn needle
- Stitch marker
- Black embroidery floss

gauge

- 6½ stitches per inch in stockinette stitch

body

Beginning at the tail end of the snake, cast on 6 stitches, placing 2 stitches on each of three double-pointed needles. Join to knit in the round, being careful not to twist the stitches. Place a stitch marker on the first stitch.

Rounds 1–6: knit

Round 7: kfb in each stitch (4 sts per needle, 12 sts total)

Round 8–19: knit

Round 20: (kfb, k2, kfb) on each needle (6 sts per needle, 18 sts total)

Round 21: (kfb, k4, kfb) on each needle
(8 sts per needle, 24 sts total)

Continue knitting every round until the snake measures 22 inches from the beginning. If you would like your snake to be longer or shorter, now is the time to make that adjustment.

Thread the tail from the cast-on stitches on a yarn needle. Stitch through all of the cast-on stitches, gather to close up the hole, and stitch to secure. Weave the end to the inside and trim. Fill the snake with stuffing after every few inches to the end.

Continue on to create the head:

Round 1:

Needle 1: knit (8 sts)

Needle 2: kfb in first 4 stitches, k4 (12 sts)

Needle 3: k4, kfb in last 4 stitches (12 sts)
 32 stitches total.

Round 2: knit

Round 3:

Needle 1: knit (8 sts)

Needle 2: kfb in first 6 sts, k6 (18 sts)

Needle 3: k6, kfb in last 6 sts (18 sts)
 44 stitches total.

Rounds 4–9: knit

Round 10:

Needle 1: knit (8 sts)

Needle 2: (k2tog) 6 times, k6 (12 sts remain)

Needle 3: k6, (k2tog) 6 times (12 sts remain)
 32 stitches total remain.

Round 11: knit

Round 12:

Needle 1: knit (8 sts)

Needle 2: (k2tog) 4 times, k4 (8 sts remain)

Needle 3: k4, (k2tog) 4 times (8 sts remain)
 24 stitches total remain.

Rounds 13–17: knit

Round 18: (k2tog), repeat across the round
(12 sts remain)

Round 19: knit

Distribute the remaining stitches on two double-pointed needles, 6 stitches on each, so that the 6 stitches that form the upper lip are on

one needle and those for the lower lip are on the other. Finish stuffing the snake. Cut the yarn, leaving an 8-inch-long tail, and thread the tail on a yarn needle. Using kitchener stitch (see p. 9), graft the mouth closed.

tongue

With two double-pointed needles used as straight needles, cast on 4 stitches. Work in I-cord (see p. 7) until the tongue measures ¾ inches from the cast-on edge.

Next row: continue in I-cord, k2 stitches; leave the other 2 stitches unworked

Work 2 rows in I-cord on these 2 stitches only.

Next row: k2tog (1 st remains)

Cut the yarn and pull through the remaining stitch.

Reattach the yarn to the 2 unworked stitches and complete the second half of the tongue in the same way as the first. Weave the bound-off tails into the tongue with a yarn needle and trim.

Thread the cast-on tail on a yarn needle and whipstitch the tongue to the mouth of the snake. Weave the tail to the inside and trim.

eyes

With black embroidery floss, take 2 small straight stitches (see p. 14) per eye. Weave all tails to the inside and trim.

finishing

To make the snake coil up, cut a length of the yarn about 18 inches long. Place the length on a yarn needle, and pull it through a stitch at the tail end. Tie a knot to secure the length. Take running stitches along the side of the snake up to the beginning of the snake's head. Pull the length gently to gather the snake up into a loose coil. Tie another knot near the snake's head and pull the end to the inside and trim. Place the knotted end near the tail on the yarn needle and pull to the inside and trim.

(5)

take-action toys

Bounce and toss, wrap and snuggle, pull and push, imagine and pretend . . . that's what you'll get with the projects in this chapter. Whenever I knit something for anyone, of any age, my hope is that it will get used and loved and squished and played with—a lot. Knits are durable and flexible and they should be used.

The following projects will take kids on a journey where they pretend and learn and interact with your knitting. I love taking a traditional toy, such as a basic pull toy, and then adding a knitted twist. It always ends up in a new place that is a lot more fun. There's something here for every level of knitter, including felted bouncy balls, graphic hand puppets, a pull toy, and some sleepy puppies to put to bed.

felted bouncy balls

I've never had more fun than when I invented this version of a felted bouncy ball. I wanted an easy, straightforward project that any beginner could make, and was thinking of some sort of felted project. I didn't want just anything, so I looked around my house for inspiration. There is kid stuff everywhere you turn, and when I spied my daughter's Super Ball, something just clicked. I quickly grabbed my needles and yarn and sat the ball in my lap as I worked. I made a small pouch, dropped the ball inside before I closed it up, then tossed the entire thing in the washing machine on hot and added a dash of detergent. I had no idea if it would work, but sure enough my crazy thoughts came to fruition.

You won't believe the bounce and feel of this fantastic toy. Instead of zooming around high and out of control, the ball's action becomes gentler and softer, much better for indoor playing. Get ready for some bouncy good fun!

finished measurements

- About 4 inches tall

yarn

- Manos Del Uruguay Handspun Semi Solids (100% kettle-dyed wool; 138 yards/100 grams); 1 skein will make several balls
- One-color balls shown in the following: Cerise 47, English E, Magenta S, Turquoise 04, French Blue 60
- Striped balls shown in the following combinations: Hollywood Pink 01/English E, Turquoise 04/French Blue 60, French Blue 60/English E
- Ball before felting shown in Spruce D

tools

- U.S. size 10.5 set of four double-pointed needles, or size needed to obtain gauge
- Bouncy ball like a Super Ball: 4-inch diameter, 8-inch circumference (see Sources)
- Tape measure
- Stitch marker
- Yarn needle
- Scissors
- Washing machine
- Laundry detergent
- Felted balls for dots (optional)
- Sewing needle and thread (optional)

gauge

- 4 stitches per inch in stockinette stitch before felting

one-color ball

With selected color, cast on 9 stitches, placing 3 stitches on each of three double-pointed needles. Join to work in the round, being careful not to twist the stitches. Place a stitch marker on the first stitch.

Round 1: knit

Round 2: kfb in each stitch (6 sts per needle, 18 sts total)

Rounds 3 and 4: knit

Round 5: kfb in each stitch (12 sts per needle, 36 sts total)

Round 6: knit

Round 7: (k1, kfb), repeat across the round (18 sts per needle, 54 sts total)

Place a stitch marker on round 7.

Knit every round until piece measures 3 inches from the stitch marker.

Decrease rounds

Round 1: (k1, k2tog), repeat across the round (12 sts per needle, 36 sts total remain)

Rounds 2 and 3: knit

Place the Super Ball inside the pouch.

Round 4: k2tog, repeat across the round
(6 sts per needle, 18 sts total remain)
Round 5: knit
Round 6: k2tog, repeat across the round
(3 sts per needle, 9 sts total remain)

Cut the yarn, leaving a 6-inch-long tail, and thread on a yarn needle. Pull through the remaining stitches, gather up tight to close the hole, and stitch to secure. Weave the end to the inside and trim. Thread the tail from the cast-on edge on a yarn needle, stitch through all of the cast-on stitches, and gather to close up the hole. Stitch to secure, weave tail to the inside, and trim.

striped ball

Work the same as for the one-color ball, alternating 2 contrasting colors every 4 rounds.
Rounds 1–4: color A
Rounds 5–8: color B

Repeat to the end of the pattern.

felting

Place the completed pouch-encased ball in the washing machine along with an old T-shirt. Add a little detergent and set the load size to small. Run the ball through the hot wash cycle as many times as needed, until the stitches are no longer visible and the felt fits snugly around the bouncy ball. Every machine and each type of yarn will felt at different rates. I ran the sample bouncy balls through the wash cycle twice.

dotted ball

After the ball is felted, take a 1 cm felted ball (see Sources) and cut it in half with a scissors. With a sewing needle and thread, whipstitch the half to the felted ball securely. Tie off the thread, pull it through the felted ball, and trim closely.

panda and zebra hand puppets

When I sat down to devise some puppets for this collection, I looked around my studio for the perfect yarn to use and immediately my eyes went straight to two skeins of Manos Del Uruguay, one of my favorite yarns. Because one skein was white and the other black, I started thinking of black and white animals—and a panda and a zebra filled the bill perfectly!

These incredibly easy and quick puppets are knit back and forth on larger-size needles. I lined the puppets with a natural wool fleece, but you could use a different fabric to line them or you could leave out this step completely. Your kids' imaginations will run "wild" with these two lovable companions.

finished measurements
- 9½ inches tall and 8½ inches wide

yarn
- Manos Del Uruguay Handspun Semi Solids (100% kettle-dyed wool; 138 yards/100 grams), 1 skein each in Natural 14 and Black 08

tools
- U.S. size 9 24-inch circular or straight needles, or size needed to obtain gauge
- Two 9- by 12-inch squares per puppet of natural-colored wool felt for lining, or fabric of your choice (optional)
- Sewing needle and matching thread (optional)
- Pins (optional)
- Scissors
- Tape measure or ruler
- yarn needle
- Small amount of fiberfill
- Crochet hook for zebra mane

gauge
- 4 stitches per inch in stockinette stitch

panda

front and back (make 2)
With Natural, cast on 26 stitches.

Knit 2 rows.

Change to working in stockinette stitch (knit 1 row, purl 1 row) until the front measures 4 inches from the cast-on edge, ending with a purl row.

Switch to Black.

Continue on to create the arms:

Next row: Knit to the end of the row, do not turn, cast on 6 stitches using the backward-loop method (32 sts). Turn.

Next row: Purl to the end of the row, do not turn, cast on 6 stitches using the backward-loop method (38 sts). Turn.

Continue to work in stockinette stitch until the arms measure 2 inches from the start of Black, ending with a purl row.

Next row: bind off 8 stitches, k to end (30 sts remain)

Next row: bind off 8 stitches, p to end (22 sts remain)

Switch to Natural.
Continue on to create the head:

Row 1: k1, ssk, k to last 3 sts, k2tog, k1 (20 sts remain)

Row 2: purl

Row 3: repeat row 1 (18 sts remain)

Row 4: purl

Continue in stockinette stitch until the head section measures 2¼ inches. End with a purl row.

Decrease rows (for the top of the head)
Row 1: k1, ssk, k to last 3 sts, k2tog, k1 (16 sts remain)
Row 2: purl
Rows 3–6: repeat rows 1 and 2 two times more (12 stitches remain)

Bind off. Cut the yarn and pull through the remaining stitch. Align the edges of the front and back pieces, purl sides facing. Lay flat, and with a length of Natural threaded on a yarn needle, use mattress stitch (see p. 10) to sew together around all edges except the bottom. Weave the ends to the inside and trim.

ears (make 2)
With Black, cast on 8 stitches.
Row 1: knit
Row 2: purl
Rows 3 and 4: repeat 1 and 2
Row 5: k2tog, repeat to end of row (4 sts remain)
Row 6: purl
Row 7: k2tog, repeat to end of row (2 sts remain)

Cut the yarn, leaving an 8-inch-long tail, and thread on a yarn needle. Pull through the remaining stitches, gather up tightly, and stitch to secure. Fold the ear in half with the purl sides together. Whipstitch the side seam from the tip to the base, using a tail. Whipstitch the ears to the top of the head, using the photograph as a guide. Weave the ends to the inside and trim.

snout
With Natural, cast on 5 stitches.
Row 1: kfb, k3, kfb (7 sts)
Row 2: purl
Row 3: kfb, k5, kfb (9 sts)
Row 4: purl
Row 5: knit
Row 6: purl
Row 7: ssk, k5, k2tog (7 sts remain)
Row 8: purl
Row 9: ssk, k3, k2tog (5 sts remain)

Bind off purlwise.

Stuff lightly and whipstitch to the face, using a length of Natural threaded on a yarn needle.

nose
With Black, cast on 1 stitch loosely.
Row 1: kfb until 3 stitches are on the right needle (3 sts)
Row 2: knit
Row 3: purl
Row 4: knit, do not turn, pass the second and third stitches over the first stitch and off the needle (1 st remains)

Cut the yarn, leaving a 6-inch-long tail, and thread on a yarn needle. Gather up the edges by taking a few stitches to create a ball, and stitch to secure. Whipstitch to the center of the nose piece.

eyes
Cut a 12-inch-long length of Black and thread on a yarn needle. Make 2 French knots (see p. 15) for the eyes. Weave ends to the inside.

lining (optional)
Lay the puppet on top of 2 layers of wool felt and pin in place. With scissors, cut out the wool felt about ⅛ inch smaller than the puppet and remove the pins. With the wool felt pieces held together and a sewing needle and matching thread, whipstitch around all edges except the bottom. Place the sewn lining inside of the puppet, wrong sides facing, and tack down the lining at the tips of the hands and the top of the head with a few stitches, using the sewing needle and thread. Whipstitch the bottom edge of the lining to the bottom edge of the puppet with the thread and needle.

zebra
front and back (make 2)
With Natural, cast on 26 stitches and begin stripe pattern. Knit the first two rows, then switch to stockinette stitch (knit 1 row, purl 1 row) for the rest of the project.

stripe pattern
Rows 1–4: Natural

Rows 5–8: Black
Repeat rows 1–8 two times more.

Continue only in Natural for the arms, and work the same as for the Panda through the bind-off rows.

Switch to Black and continue in stripes, alternating every 4 rows and complete the head the same as for the Panda.

face and snout (make 1)
With Black, cast on 12 stitches.
Row 1: k1, m1, k to last stitch, m1, k1 (14 sts)
Row 2: purl
Row 3: repeat row 1 (16 sts)
Row 4: purl

Switch to Natural.
Row 5: repeat row 1 (18 sts)
Row 6: purl
Row 7: knit
Row 8: purl

Switch to Black.
Rows 9–12: stockinette stitch

Switch to Natural.
Rows 13–16: stockinette stitch

Switch to Black.
Rows 17–20: stockinette stitch

Switch to Natural.
Rows 21–28: stockinette stitch

Switch to Black.
Rows 29–32: stockinette stitch

Switch to Natural.
Rows 33 and 34: stockinette stitch
Row 35: k1, ssk, k to the last 3 stitches, k2tog, k1 (16 sts remain)
Row 36: purl

Switch to Black.
Row 37: repeat row 35 (14 sts remain)

Row 38: purl
Row 39: repeat row 35 (12 sts remain)
Row 40: purl

Bind off. Cut the yarn and weave through the remaining stitch.

ears (make 2)
With Natural, cast on 14 stitches. Work in stockinette stitch until the ear measures 1 inch from the cast-on edge.

Decrease rows
Row 1: k1, ssk, k3, k2tog, k3, k2tog, k1
(11 sts remain)
Row 2: purl
Row 3: k1, ssk, k1, k2tog, k2, k2tog, k1
(8 sts remain)
Row 4: p1, p2tog, p2, p2tog, p1 (6 sts remain)
Row 5: k1, ssk, k2tog, k1 (4 sts remain)
Row 6: p2tog twice, do not turn, pass the first stitch over the second stitch and off the needle. Cut the yarn, leaving a 6-inch-long tail, and thread on a yarn needle. Fold the ear in half with the purl sides together and whipstitch the open side closed from the base to the tip. Set aside.

lining (optional)
Make the lining the same as for the Panda, but don't sew the pieces together yet. In addition to cutting the lining for the front and back, also pin down the face and snout piece on 1 layer of the wool felt and cut out a lining for it. Set aside.

finish the front and back
Lay the front and back of the knitted pieces on top of each other, with purl sides facing. With a length of Natural threaded on a yarn needle, use mattress stitch to sew the side seams together to where the head starts.

Fold the front of the head forward to rest on the body, using the illustration as a guide. This is now the bottom of the snout. Leave the back of the head as is. Lay the face and snout piece on top of the folded front and align with the back of the head, purl sides together.

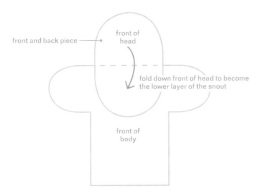

front and back piece

front of head

fold down front of head to become the lower layer of the snout

front of body

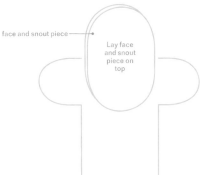

face and snout piece

Lay face and snout piece on top

Thread a length of Natural on a yarn needle and use mattress stitch to sew the face and nose piece to the bottom of the nose and the back of the head.

After the head and nose are sewn together, whipstitch the ears to the head, using the photograph as a guide.

nostrils and eyes

With Natural and a yarn needle, make 2 French knots (see p. 00) at the tip of the nose for the nostrils. With Black and a yarn needle, take 2 straight stitches with 4 wrap stitches and a French knot underneath for each eye (see pp. 00). Weave all ends to the inside and trim.

finish the lining

With a sewing needle and matching thread, whipstitch the front and back pieces together from the lower edges up to the base of the head. Fold the front piece forward for the bottom of the snout and lay the cutout face and snout piece on top so it lines up evenly. Pin in place. Continue to whipstitch the head and nose pieces together. The lining is the same shape as the puppet.

Lightly stuff the head of the lining with fiberfill, and with a needle and thread stitch with a running stitch (see p. 00) to hold the stuffing in place. Leave the snout open so that the puppeteer can put his or her fingers into it.

Place the lining in the puppet, making sure that the nose of the lining is pushed into the nose of the knitted front. Tack down at the tip of the

hands, the end of the snout, and the top of the head with a few stitches with the sewing needle and thread. With the sewing needle and thread, whipstitch the bottom edge of the lining to the bottom edge of the puppet. Weave the ends of the thread to the inside and trim.

mane

With Black, cut 96 3-inch strands. Holding two strands together at a time, use to make fringe. With a crochet hook and the lengths folded in half, pull the looped end through and then pull the ends through the loop. Pull up tight. Fringe is through 3 stitches in a row between the ears, then continue in a straight line down through the stripe section on the back of the head. The sample has 16 rows with three fringes per row.

mama duck and ducklings

I love pull toys, and I love to see toddlers pulling one even more. They are traditionally offered in stores in wooden and plush versions, but I've never seen a knitted version.

These ducks are constructed in a fantastic way, starting with a simple base knitted back and forth. To make the body, stitches are picked up around the base edge and knitted up from there. The body, head, and tail are all knitted in one piece, and it is so fun to see the ducks take shape as you work.

I provided instructions for duck feet for those who don't want to make the wheels, but the wheels are not at all difficult to construct. I have no woodworking skills whatsoever, but I made, cut, and assembled the wheels on the kitchen counter. The result? Sitting still or rolling along, these ducks are as cute as can be.

finished measurements

- Ducklings: 3 inches tall, 5 inches long from beak to tail
- Mama duck: 5 inches tall, 8 inches long from beak to tail

yarn

- Blue Sky Dyed Cotton (100% organically grown cotton; 150 yards/100 grams), 2 skeins in Lemonade #608 and Honeydew #602, 1 skein in Pumpkin #622

tools

- U.S. size 5 set of four double-pointed needles, or size needed to obtain gauge
- Scissors
- Tape measure or ruler
- Stitch markers
- 2 stitch holders
- Yarn needle
- Polyester fiberfill, 1 small bag
- Black embroidery floss

to add optional wheels

- Wheels
- 2 ¾-inch dowels (cherrywood is shown)
- Saw
- Sandpaper
- Drill
- ³⁄₁₆-inch drill bit
- 12 axles (pegs to hold wheels)
- 4 1¾-inch wheels (for Mama)
- 8 1½-inch wheels (for Ducklings)
- Wood glue
- Hammer

mama duck

bottom

With Lemonade and two double-pointed needles used as straight needles, cast on 5 stitches.

Row 1: kfb, k to the last stitch, kfb (7 sts)
Row 2 and every following even row: purl
Row 3: kfb, k to the last stitch, kfb (9 sts)
Row 5: kfb, k to the last stitch, kfb (11 sts)

Continue to work in stockinette stitch (knit 1 row, purl 1 row) until the bottom measures 3½ inches from the cast-on edge, ending with a purl row.

Decrease rows
Row 1: ssk, k to last 2 stitches, k2tog (9 sts remain)
Row 2: purl
Row 3: ssk, k2 to last 2 stitches, k2tog (7 sts remain)
Row 4: ssk, k to last 2 stitches, k2tog (5 sts remain)

Place a stitch marker on the first of these 5 stitches. Continue on from the 5 stitches already on the needle and pick up (see p. 8) 40 more stitches around the bottom. As you pick up, place 15 stitches on each of three double-pointed needles (45 stitches total).

Begin working in the round to create the body:

First round: knit

Next round: (k3, m1), repeat to end of round (20 sts per needle, 60 sts total)

Knit every round until the body measures 3 inches from the pickup round.

Continue on to create the tail:

Knit the first 7 stitches. Place the next 48 stitches on a couple of stitch holders. There will be 5 stitches remaining at the end. You will be working on the first 7 stitches and the last 5 stitches (12 stitches). Knit across the 5 stitches. Arrange these 12 stitches by placing 4 stitches on each of three double-pointed needles. Begin working in the round.

Rounds 1–3: knit

Round 4: (k2, k2tog), repeat on each needle (3 sts per needle, 9 sts total remain)

Round 5: (k1, k2tog), repeat on each needle (2 sts per needle, 6 sts total remain)

Round 6: k2tog, repeat on each needle (1 st per needle, 3 sts total remain)

Cut the yarn and thread on a yarn needle. Pull through the remaining stitches, gather up tight to close the hole, and stitch to secure. Weave the end to the inside and trim.

Continue on to create the top of the back:

Working from the tail end, place 14 stitches on one double-pointed needle. Place the next 20 stitches on a stitch holder. Place the final 14 stitches on one double-pointed needle. Stuff the body and tail with fiberfill.

With a length of Lemonade and a yarn needle, use kitchener stitch (see p. 9) to graft the top of the back. Use the tail to close the gap between the duck's tail and back by taking a couple of stitches with a yarn needle. Weave the ends to the inside and trim.

Continue on to create the head:

Reattach Lemonade to the back to start working the remaining 20 stitches. Leave a long tail to use later to close the gap. Place the 20 stitches on three double-pointed needles as follows:

Needles 1 and 2: 6 sts

Needle 3: 8 sts

Place a stitch marker on the first stitch.

Round 1: knit

Round 2:

Needles 1 and 2: (k2, m1, k2, m1, k2), repeat on each needle (8 sts per needle)

Needle 3: k2, m1, k2, m1, k2, m1, k2 (11 sts)

27 sts total

Round 3: knit

Round 4:

Needles 1 and 2: ([k2, m1] repeat 3 times, k2) on each needle (11 sts)

Needle 3: (k2, m1) repeat 5 times, k1 (16 sts)

38 sts total

Rounds 5–14: knit

Round 15: ([k3, k2tog] repeat to last stitch, k1) on each needle

Needles 1 and 2: 9 sts each

Needle 3: 13 sts

31 sts total remain

Round 16: (k1, k2tog), repeat to the last stitch, k1

Needles 1 and 2: 6 sts each

Needle 3: 9 sts

21 sts total remain

Round 17: knit

Round 18: (k1, k2tog), repeat to end of round

Needles 1 and 2: 4 sts each

Needle 3: 6 sts

14 sts total remain

Stuff the head with fiberfill.

Round 19: knit

Round 20: k2tog, repeat to end of round

Needles 1 and 2: 2 sts each

Needle 3: 3 sts

7 sts total remain

Cut the yarn and thread the tail on a yarn needle. Pull through the remaining stitches, gather up tight to close the hole, and stitch to secure. Weave the end to the inside and trim. Thread the tail from the reattached yarn into the yarn needle. Close the gap between the head and the back seam with a few stitches. Weave the end to the inside and trim.

wings

upper wing (make 2)

With Lemonade and two double-pointed needles used as straight needles, cast on 3 stitches.

Row 1: k1, m1, k1, m1, k1 (5 sts)

Row 2 and every following even row: purl

Row 3: k1, m1, k3, m1, k1 (7 sts)

Row 5: k1, m1, k5, m1, k1 (9 sts)

Rows 7, 9, and 11: knit

Row 13: k1, ssk, k3, k2tog, k1 (7 sts)

Row 15: k1, ssk, k1, k2tog, k1 (5 sts)

Row 17: k1, ssk, k2tog (3 sts)

Row 19: sl1, k2tog, pass the slipped stitch over and off the right needle (1 st remains)

Cut the yarn and pull the end through the remaining stitch.

underside of wing (make 2)

With Pumpkin and two double-pointed needles used as straight needles, cast on 3 stitches.

Rows 1–4: same as for the upper wing

Rows 7–12: same as for the upper wing

Rows 15–19: same as for the upper wing

Cut the yarn and pull the end through the remaining stitch.

Place one upper wing piece on each underside wing piece, purl sides together. With a yarn needle and the bound-off tails from the upper wings, whipstitch the edges of the wings together. Whipstitch the wings to the back of the duck, using the photograph as a guide.

beak

With Pumpkin, cast on 16 stitches and place the stitches on three double-pointed needles as follows:

Needles 1 and 2: 5 sts each

Needle 3: 6 sts

Join to work in the round, being careful not to twist the stitches. Place a stitch marker on the first stitch. Knit every round until the beak measures 1 inch from the cast-on edge.

Decrease rounds

Round 1: ssk, k4, k2tog, ssk, k4, k2tog (12 sts remain)

Round 2: ssk, k2, k2tog, ssk, k2, k2tog (8 sts remain)

Round 3: ssk, k to last 2 sts, k2tog (6 sts remain)

Divide the remaining stitches and arrange on two double-pointed needles so the 3 stitches that make up the upper beak are on one needle, and the lower beak stitches are on the other. Cut the yarn, leaving an 8-inch-long tail, and thread on a yarn needle. Use kitchener stitch to graft the end of the beak. Weave the tail to the inside. Stuff the beak lightly with fiberfill. Whipstitch the beak to the head with a length of Lemonade and weave in ends.

eyes

With black embroidery floss and a yarn needle, take small straight stitches (see p. 14) for each eye on each side of the head, using the photograph as a guide. Weave the ends to the inside and trim.

feet (make 2)

If you are making the ducks into a pull toy, do not make the feet. If you prefer not to make the wheels, make two duck feet for the front of the duck as follows:

With Pumpkin, cast on 10 stitches and arrange the stitches on three double-pointed needles as follows:

Needles 1 and 2: 3 sts each

Needle 3: 4 sts

Join to work in the round, being careful not to twist the stitches. Place a stitch marker on the first stitch.

Round 1: knit

Round 2: k1, m1, k to the last stitch, m1, k1 (12 sts)

Knit every round until the foot measures ¾ inch from the cast-on edge. Rearrange the stitches on two double-pointed needles so that the 6 stitches that make up the top of the foot are on one needle and the bottom of the foot are on the other. Cut the yarn, leaving an 8-inch-long tail, and thread on a yarn needle. Use kitchener stitch to graft the end of the foot. Weave the tail to the inside and trim. Stuff the feet lightly with fiberfill. Whipstitch the back end of the feet with the cast-on tails threaded on a yarn needle. With a length of Lemonade threaded on a yarn needle, whipstitch the feet to the bottom of the duck so the feet stick out and the duck can stand. Use the photograph on page 95 as a guide.

duckling (make 2)

bottom

With Lemonade and two double-pointed needles used as straight needles, cast on 3 stitches.

Row 1: kfb, k1, kfb (5 sts)

Row 2: purl

Row 3: kfb, k3, kfb (7 sts)

Continue to work in stockinette stitch until the bottom piece measures 1¾ inches from the cast-on edge. End with a purl row.

Decrease rows

Row 1: ssk, k3, k2tog (5 sts remain)

Row 2: purl

Row 3: ssk, k1, k2tog (3 sts remain)

Continue on to create the body:

Working from the 3 stitches already on the needle, begin picking up stitches around the bottom piece. Pick up 24 more stitches, placing 9 stitches on each of three double-pointed needles as you pick up. (9 sts per needle, 27 sts total).

Place a stitch marker on the first stitch of the first needle and knit 1 round.

Next round: (k2, m1), repeat to the last stitch, k1, on each needle (13 sts per needle, 39 sts total)

Knit every round until the body measures 2 inches from the pickup round.

Continue on to create the tail:

Knit the first 4 stitches, place the next 31 stitches on stitch holders, knit the last 4 stitches. Place these 8 stitches on three double-pointed needles as follows:

Needles 1 and 2: 3 sts each

Needle 3: 2 sts

Rounds 1 and 2: knit

Round 3: (k1, k2tog) 2 times, k2 (6 sts remain)

Round 4: k2tog on each needle (3 sts remain)

Cut the yarn and thread the end on a yarn needle. Pull through the remaining stitches, pull up tight to close the hole, and stitch to secure. Weave the end to the inside.

Stuff the body and the tail with fiberfill.

Continue on to create the top of the back:

Starting at the tail end, place the first 9 stitches on one double-pointed needle, place the next 13 stitches on a stitch holder, place the final 9 stitches on one double-pointed needle. With a length of Lemonade threaded on a yarn needle, use kitchener stitch to graft the seam along the back, leaving the 13 stitches on the holder free.

Take a few stitches to close the gap between the seam and the tail.

Continue on to create the head:

Reattach Lemonade to the last stitch held on the stitch holder, leaving a long tail for seaming the gap later. Arrange the 13 stitches on three double-pointed needles as follows:

Needles 1 and 2: 4 sts each

Needle 3: 5 sts

Place a stitch marker on the first stitch.

Round 1: knit

Round 2:

Needles 1 and 2: k1, m1, k1, m1, k2 (6 sts)

Needle 3: k1, m1, k1, m1, k1, m1, k2 (8 sts)

20 stitches total.

Round 3: knit

Round 4:

Needles 1 and 2: (k2, m1) repeat twice, k2 (8 sts)

Needle 3: (k2, m1) repeat three times, k2 (11 sts)

27 stitches total.

Place 9 stitches on each double-pointed needle.

Rounds 5–11: knit

Decrease rounds

Round 12: (k2, k2tog), repeat twice, k1, on each needle (7 sts per needle, 21 sts total remain)

Round 13: (k1, k2tog), repeat twice, k1, on each needle (5 sts per needle, 15 sts total remain)

Stuff the head with fiberfill.

Round 14: knit

Round 15: k2tog, repeat twice, k1 (3 sts per needle, 9 sts total remain)

Cut the yarn and thread on a yarn needle. Pull through the remaining stitches, pull up tight to close the hole, and stitch to secure. Weave the end to the inside and trim. Thread the tail from the reattached yarn into the yarn needle and take a few stitches to close the gap between the back seam and the head. Weave the end to the inside and trim.

wings

upper wing (make 2 per duckling)

With Lemonade and two double-pointed needles used as straight needles, cast on 3 stitches.

Row 1: k1, m1, k1, m1, k1 (5 sts)

Row 2 and every following even row: purl

Rows 3, 5, 7, 9, and 11: knit

Row 13: ssk, k1, k2tog (3 sts remain)

Row 15: sl1, k2tog, pass the slipped stitch over the first stitch and off the needle (1 st remains)

Cut the yarn and pull the end through the remaining stitch.

underside of wing (make 2 per duckling)

With Pumpkin, complete as for the upper wing.

Complete and attach the wings the same as for the Mama Duck.

duckling beak

With Pumpkin, cast on 12 stitches, placing 4 stitches on each of three double-pointed needles. Join to work in the round, being careful not to twist the stitches. Place a stitch marker on the first stitch.

Knit every round until the beak measures ¾ inch from the cast-on edge.

Decrease rounds

Round 1: (ssk, k2, k2tog), repeat to end of round (8 sts remain)

Round 2: (ssk, k2tog), repeat to end of round (4 sts remain)

Arrange the remaining stitches so that the 2 stitches that make up the upper beak are on one double-pointed needle, and the lower beak stitches are on the other. Cut the yarn, leaving an 8-inch-long tail, and use kitchener stitch to graft the end of the beak. Weave the end to the inside and trim. Stuff lightly with fiberfill and use the tail from the cast-on edge to whipstitch the beak to the duckling's head.

feet (make 2 per duckling)

If you are making the ducks into a pull toy, do not make the feet. If you prefer not to make the wheels, make 2 duck feet for the front of the ducklings as follows:

With Pumpkin, cast on 8 stitches and place the stitches on three double-pointed needles as follows:

Needles 1 and 2: 3 sts each

Needle 3: 2 sts

Join to work in the round, being careful not to twist the stitches. Place a stitch marker on the first stitch.

Round 1: knit

Round 2: k1, m1, k to the last stitch, m1, k1 (10 sts)

Knit every round until the foot measures ½ inch from the cast-on edge. Arrange the remaining stitches so that the 5 stitches that make up the top of the foot are on one double-pointed needle, and those for the bottom are on the other. Cut the yarn, leaving an 8-inch-long tail, and thread on a yarn needle. Use kitchener stitch to graft the end of the foot. Weave the tail to the inside and trim. Stuff lightly with fiberfill. Whipstitch the cast-on end closed. With a length of Lemonade threaded on a yarn needle, whipstitch the feet to the bottom of each duckling so they stick out and the duckling can stand. Use the photograph as a guide.

wheels (optional)

If you choose to make your ducks into pull toys, begin by making the cords that attach the wheels to the bottom of each duck.

wheel cords (make 12)

With Pumpkin and two double-pointed needles used as straight needles, cast on 3 stitches. Work in I-cord (see p. 7) for 1¾ inches. Bind off. Cut the yarn, leaving a 6-inch-long tail, and pull through the remaining stitch. Set aside.

wheel axles

Begin by cutting the dowels with a saw. An extra pair of hands to hold the dowel steady helps here if you don't have a clamp. For the Mama Duck, cut the dowel into two 2-inch pieces. For the Ducklings, cut the dowel into four 1¾-inch pieces. Sand the ends.

With a drill and the ³⁄₁₆-inch drill bit, drill a ½-inch hole into each end of all the dowel pieces.

mama duck wheels

Use the four 1¾-inch wheels. Put a drop of wood glue into the holes in the wheel before gently hammering the axles into the wheels. Repeat on each end.

duckling wheels

Complete the wheels the same as for the Mama Duck, but use the 1¾-inch dowel pieces and the 1½-inch wheels.

attaching the wheels

The process of attaching the wheels is the same for the Mama Duck and the Ducklings. With a length of Pumpkin threaded on a yarn needle, hold the dowel to the bottom of the duck where you want to place it. Take several stitches over the dowel and through the bottom of the duck. Complete these stitches in two different spots for each dowel. Place the wheel cord pieces over the stitches and tack down the ends. Weave all ends to the inside and trim.

pull cord

With Honeydew and two double-pointed needles used as straight needles, cast on 3 stitches.

Working in I-cord, make 3 cords in the following lengths:

Cord 1: 23 inches
Cord 2: 5 inches
Cord 3: 4 inches

When each cord measures the desired length, bind off, leaving a 6-inch-long tail. Cut the yarn and pull through the remaining stitch.

Using the bound-off tail threaded on a yarn needle, whipstitch cord 1 to the front of the mama duck. Use the photograph as a guide. At the other end, make a loop big enough to fit a little hand. Tack down the end with a few stitches, using the cast-on tail. Weave the end through the cord and trim.

In the same manner, attach one end from cord 2 to the front of one of the ducklings and the other end to the tail end of the mama duck.

Attach cord 3 to the front of the remaining duckling and the tail end of the first duckling.

wrap-me-up puppies

All small children like to pretend to put their toys or dolls to bed. At my house, when the kids were little, we would put the dolls, stuffed monkeys, and teddy bears "night, night" all day long. Then the toys wake up and the kids want to do it all over again.

I made these sweet little puppies with this universal activity in mind. Each sleepy puppy has its own little blanket to be wrapped up in, and the blanket has a bobble button to hold it in place. Have fun wrapping up these sleepy puppies along with the little one in your life.

finished measurements

- Puppies: 6½ inches long (including tail), 2½ inches wide
- Blankets: 7 x 7 inches

yarn

- Blue Sky Alpacas Skinny Dyed (100% organically grown cotton; 150 yards/65 grams), 1 skein each in Glacier #301, Coffee #310, and Pink #305
- Blue Sky Alpacas Skinny Organic (100% organic cotton; 150 yards/65 grams), 1 skein in Clay #31

tools

- Puppies: U.S. size 3 set of four double-pointed needles, or size needed to obtain gauge
- Blanket: U.S. size 5 needles or size needed to obtain gauge
- U.S. size G crochet hook (optional)
- Tape measure or ruler
- Scissors
- Stitch markers
- Yarn needle
- Polyester fiberfill, 1 small bag
- Poly pellets (optional), 32-ounce bag
- Black, pink, and tan embroidery floss
- 8 x 8 inch piece of fabric (optional)
- Sewing needle and matching thread (optional)
- Pins (optional)

body

With Clay or Coffee, cast on 9 stitches, placing 3 stitches on each of three double-pointed needles. Join to work in the round, being careful not to twist the stitches. Place a stitch marker on the first stitch.

Round 1: knit

Round 2: (k1, m1, k1, m1, k1), repeat on each needle (5 sts per needle, 15 sts total)

Round 3: knit

Round 4: (k1, [m1, k1] three times, k1), repeat on each needle (8 sts per needle, 24 sts total)

Round 5: knit

Round 6: (k1, m1, k to last stitch, m1, k1), repeat on each needle (10 sts per needle, 30 sts total)

Round 7: repeat round 6 (12 sts per needle, 36 sts total)

Rounds 8–19: knit

Round 20: k20, k2tog, k2tog, ssk, ssk, k8

Needle 1: 12 sts (needle 1 becomes the bottom of the body)

Needles 2 and 3: 10 sts each
    32 stitches total remain.

Rounds 21–35: knit

Continue on to create the neck and head:

Round 36:

Needle 1: (k2, k2tog), repeat three times (9 sts remain)

Needles 2 and 3: (k2, k2tog), repeat twice (8 sts remain)
    25 stitches total remain.

Rounds 37 and 38: knit

Round 39:
Needle 1: knit (9 sts)
Needles 2 and 3: (k1, [m1, k1] repeat 6 times, k1) on each needle (14 sts per needle)
　　37 sts total remain.
Round 40: knit
Round 41:
Needle 1: knit (9 sts)
Needles 2 and 3: (k3, m1, k8, m1, k3) on each needle (16 sts per needle)
　　41 sts total.
Rounds 42–47: knit

Thread the tail from the cast-on edge on a yarn needle. Stitch through all of the cast-on stitches, gather to close the hole, and stitch to secure. Weave the end to the inside and trim. Stuff firmly to the top with fiberfill.

Continue on to create the face and nose:
Decrease rounds
Round 1:
Needle 1: knit (9 sts)
Needle 2: k8, (k2tog) four times (12 sts remain)
Needle 3: (k2tog) four times, k8 (12 sts remain)
　　33 sts total remain.
Round 2:
Needle 1: knit (9 sts)
Needle 2: k6, (k2tog) three times (9 sts remain)
Needle 3: (k2tog) three times, k6 (9 sts remain)
　　27 sts total remain.
Round 3:
Needle 1: ssk, k5, k2tog (7 sts remain)
Needles 2 and 3: knit (9 sts per needle)
　　25 sts total remain.
Round 4: knit
Round 5:
Needle 1: knit (7 sts)
Needles 2 and 3: k1, ssk, k3, k2tog, k1 (7 sts remain)
　　21 sts total remain.
Round 6: knit
Round 7: (k1, ssk, k1, k2tog, k1), repeat on each needle (5 sts per needle, 15 sts total remain)
Round 8: knit

Round 9: (k3, k2tog), repeat on each needle (4 sts per needle, 12 sts total remain)
　　Finish stuffing.
Round 10: (k2, k2tog), repeat on each needle (3 sts per needle, 9 sts total remain)

　　Cut the yarn and thread the tail on a yarn needle. Pull through the remaining stitches, gather up tight to close the hole, and stitch to secure. Weave the end to the inside and trim.

ears (make 2 for each puppy)
With Clay or Coffee, cast on 9 stitches and place 3 stitches on each of three double-pointed needles. Join to work in the round, being careful not to twist the stitches. Place a stitch marker on the first stitch.
Rounds 1–3: knit
Round 4: (k1, m1, k2), repeat on each needle (4 sts per needle, 12 sts total)
Rounds 5 and 6: knit
Round 7: ssk, k2, k2tog, ssk, k2, k2tog (8 sts total remain)

　　Redistribute 4 stitches each on needle 1 and needle 3. Cut the yarn, leaving an 8-inch-long tail. Thread on a yarn needle and use kitchener stitch (see p. 9) to graft the end of the ear.

Thread the tail from the cast-on stitches on a yarn needle and whipstitch the ears to the head. Weave the ends to the inside and trim.

back legs (make 2 for each puppy)
With Clay or Coffee, cast on 12 stitches, placing 4 stitches on each of three double-pointed needles. Join to work in the round, being careful not to twist the stitches. Place a stitch marker on the first stitch.
　　Knit every round until the leg measures 1 inch from the cast-on stitches.
Next round: (k1, m1, k2, m1, k1) on each needle (6 sts per needle, 18 sts total)
　　Knit 5 rounds.
Next round: (k1, k2tog), repeat to end of round (4 sts per needle, 12 sts total remain)
Next round: (k2tog) repeat to end of round (2 sts per needle, 6 sts total remain)

finishing

Cut the yarn, leaving a 6-inch-long tail, and thread on a yarn needle. Pull through the remaining stitches, pull up tight to close the hole, and stitch to secure. Either fill the paw with poly pellets and stuff the leg with fiberfillaZpo[pp[fdxgor stuff both with fiberfill only.

Thread the tail from the cast-on stitches on a yarn needle. Whipstitch the cast-on edge closed. Whipstitch the back legs to the rear underside of the body so the legs stick out at an angle, using the photograph as a guide.

front legs (make 2 for each puppy)

With Clay or Coffee, cast on 9 stitches, placing 3 stitches on each of three double-pointed needles. Join to work in the round, being careful not to twist the stitches. Place a stitch marker on the first stitch.

Knit every round until the leg measures 1 inch from the cast-on edge.

Next round: (k1, m1, k2), repeat on each needle (4 sts per needle, 12 sts total)

Knit 3 rounds.

Next round: (k2, k2tog) on each needle (3 sts per needle, 9 sts total remain)

Next round: (k1, k2tog) on each needle (2 sts per needle, 6 sts total remain)

Finish as for the back legs, but attach the legs to the front underside of the body.

tail (make 1 for each puppy)

With Clay or Coffee, cast on 9 stitches, placing 3 stitches on each of three double-pointed needles. Join to work in the round, being careful not to twist the stitches. Place a stitch marker on the first stitch.

Knit every round until the tail measures 1 inch from the cast-on edge.

Next round: (k1, k2tog) on each needle (2 sts per needle, 6 sts total remain)

Knit 2 rounds.

Cut the yarn, leaving a 6-inch-long tail, and thread on a yarn needle. Pull through the remaining stitches, gather up tight to close the hole, and stitch to secure. Stuff lightly with fiberfill. Thread the tail from the cast-on stitches on a yarn needle and whipstitch the tail to the back end of the body.

nose and eyes

With pink (for the Coffee puppy) or black (for the Clay puppy) embroidery floss and a yarn needle, use satin stitch (see p. 14) to create a nose. Weave the ends to the inside and trim.

With black (for the Clay puppy) or tan (for the Coffee puppy) embroidery floss and a yarn needle, take 2 small straight stitches (see p. 14) for the eyes. Weave the ends to the inside and trim.

blanket (make 1 for each puppy)

blanket (make 1 for each puppy)

There are two versions of the blankets; both are worked in the same way, but have different colors and edgings.

With Pink or Glacier and the larger needles, cast on 36 stitches.
Work in double seed stitch as follows:

Rows 1 and 2: (k2, p2), repeat to end of row
Rows 3 and 4: (p2, k2), repeat to end of row
    Repeat rows 1–4 until the blanket measures 6 inches, ending with row 2 or row 4.
    Bind off, leaving the last stitch on the needle.

Choose whether to edge the blanket or not; the blanket will lie flat with or without the crochet edging. The samples are made in Glacier and Coffee or Pink.

crocheted edging (optional, see page 12)

Place the crochet hook in the remaining stitch.
Round 1: Chain 1, single crochet around the edge, placing 3 single crochet stitches in each corner. Slip stitch the first and last stitches together.
Round 2: Chain 3, double crochet in each stitch, placing 3 double crochet stitches in each corner.
    On the last corner, chain 10 stitches and slip stitch to the first stitch to form a loop.

garter stitch edging (optional)

Do not bind off the stitches. Switch to Coffee.
    Knit 6 rows. Bind off and leave the last stitch on the needle. Turn clockwise to work down the next side.
    Pick up (see p. 8) 35 sts on the next side (36 sts total on the needle). Knit 5 rows. Bind off and leave the remaining stitch on the needle. Turn clockwise to work down the next side.
    Pick up 38 sts (39 sts total on the needle). Knit 5 rows. Bind off and leave the last stitch on the needle. Turn clockwise to work on the last side.
    Pick up 38 sts (39 sts total on the needle). Knit 5 rows. Bind off and leave the last stitch on the needle.
    Button loop: Using the backward-loop method, cast on 9 stitches. Bind off. Cut the yarn and thread on a yarn needle. Whipstitch the end to the first stitch to form a loop.
    Weave in all ends and trim.

Give either version of the blanket a good steam to block.

fabric backing (optional)

Pin the blanket to the piece of fabric. Cut around the blanket, leaving a ¼-inch seam allowance on all sides.
    Pin the fabric to the blanket, turning under the ¼-inch seam allowance toward the wrong side as you go. With the needle and thread, whipstitch the fabric to the blanket around all sides. Knot and weave the thread to the inside and trim.

bobble for a button

With Pink or Coffee, cast on 1 stitch loosely, leaving a 2-inch-long tail.
Row 1: kfb until 5 stitches are on the right needle (5 sts)
Row 2: knit
Row 3: purl
Row 4: knit, do not turn, pull the second, third, fourth, and fifth stitches over the first stitch and off the needle.
    Cut the yarn, leaving a 6-inch-long tail, and thread on a yarn needle. Stuff the bobble with the tail from the cast-on stitch. With the tail and yarn needle, take a few stitches on the edges of the bobble, gather up, and close to form a ball. Sew the bobble to the back side of the blanket so the loop can catch the bobble and hold the blanket closed.

Optional: If you lined the blanket with fabric, use a sewing needle and thread to stitch the puppy to the center of the nonbobble side of the blanket, at the puppy's tummy, using the photograph as a guide. If you have not used fabric, use a length of yarn threaded on a yarn needle. Weave in all ends and trim.

6

classic toys revisited

I often get nostalgic for the good old days, when there were only three channels on the television, there was no such thing as a video game, and your imagination was your best friend. Those of you who grew up in that kind of environment know how much toys can mean to a child.

For the Classic Toy collection, I drew upon my memory of classic toys and classic characters, all of which you will recognize. Each has a place in history and they are all popular in our current cultures in one way or another.

I've included matryoshka dolls (they've been a classic in Russia for generations, and have become very popular in North America in recent years), a Christmas set to play with and cherish year after year, a baby doll with clothes and a matching child's hat (I had to sneak at least one in), and in tribute to my favorite fairy tale, a princess and a pea. All of these toys are keepers and will be adored for years to come. I bet you can't wait to get started.

princess and the pea

I started knitting this set on a long car trip with my family. The kids were all very interested in my progress as we drove east on our summer vacation. I started by knitting five mattresses, which I thought was enough. But my kids were disappointed there weren't more. I agreed with them that there should be lots to stack, so I continued making mattresses until I reached eleven—then everyone was happy.

Nevertheless, you could make one, two, or three mattresses and your set will still be fun. Little ones will love stacking them up extra-high and putting the princess to bed. And I've included a nightie and blanket to help with the bedtime ritual.

The princess is a simple little doll, and she is beautiful on her own if you are looking for a quick, easy project. Her legs, body, and head are made in one piece and the arms are added on. I stuffed the princess with natural wool roving to give her substance.

The entire set is made in a beautiful worsted-weight wool blend yarn that gives it a rustic feel. The pea pod is storybook-like itself and adds the final touch to the set. This project is a dream come true for me, something I have longed to design for many years.

finished measurements

- Large mattresses: 5 x 7 inches
- Small mattresses: 3½ x 6 inches
- Princess: 7½ inches tall
- Blanket: 6 x 6 inches
- Pea pod: 4½ inches long

yarn

- Nashua Handknits Julia (50% wool, 25% alpaca, 25% kid mohair; 93 yards/50grams), 1 skein each in Aqua Fog #4013, Blue Thyme #4936, Geranium #6085, Persimmon #0121, Natural #0010, Rose #1715, and Celery #5293; 2 skeins each in Golden Honey #2163, Rock Henna #2230, and Spring Green #5185

tools

- Mattresses: U.S. size 6 needles, or size needed to obtain gauge
- Princess: U.S. size 5 set of four double-pointed needles, or size needed to obtain gauge
- Blanket and nightgown: U.S. size 7 set of four double-pointed needles and either 24-inch circular needle or straight needles, or size needed to obtain gauge

- U.S. size G crochet hook (optional)
- 2 sheets of 15- x 17-inch 1-inch-thick foam
- Stitch holder
- Stitch markers
- Yarn needle
- Scissors
- Tape measure or ruler
- Natural wool roving for stuffing
- 1 cm green wool felt balls for peas (optional)
- 1 green pipe cleaner
- Black and red embroidery floss
- Sewing needle and green thread

gauge

- 5½ stitches per inch in stockinette stitch for the mattresses
- 6 stitches per inch in stockinette stitch for the princess
- 5 stitches per inch in stockinette stitch for the blanket and the nightgown

large mattress (make 6)

The large mattress samples were worked in the following color combinations:

Mattress 1 side 1: Aqua Fog;
               side 2: Blue Thyme
Mattress 2 side 1: Geranium;
               side 2: Golden Honey
Mattress 3 side 1: Blue Thyme;
               side 2:Persimmon
Mattress 4 side 1: Persimmon;
               side 2:Geranium
Mattress 5 side 1: Rock Henna;
               side 2: Aqua Fog
Mattress 6 side 1: Natural;
               side 2: Rose

With size 6 needles, or the size needed to obtain gauge, and the selected color, cast on 30 stitches. Work in stockinette stitch (knit 1 row, purl 1 row) until the mattress measures 7¼ inches from the cast-on edge, ending with a purl row. Bind off. Cut the yarn and pull through the remaining stitch. Steam the sides and let dry.

Cut six 4¾ x 7 inch pieces of foam.

crocheted edging (optional)

With the crochet hook and Spring Green, single crochet (see p. 12) in every stitch around the edge of the mattress, working 3 single crochet stitches in each of the four corners.

Hold the two selected sides together with the purl sides facing, and slip stitch (see p. 12) the edges together, leaving one short end open. Slide a foam rectangle into the mattress piece. Continue closing the final edge with slip stitch. Cut the yarn, pull through the last stitch, and weave the yarn to the inside. Trim.

alternate mattress assembly

Hold the two selected sides with the purl sides together, and with an end threaded on a yarn needle, use mattress stitch (see p. 10) to seam the edges together, leaving one short end open. Place the cut foam inside and close the final edge with mattress stitch. Cut the yarn, weave the end to the inside, and stitch to secure. Trim.

small mattress (make 5)

The small mattress samples were made in the following color combinations:

Mattress 1 side 1: Golden Honey; side 2: Rose
Mattress 2 side 1: Natural; side 2: Rock Henna
Mattress 3 side 1: Stripe pattern in Rock Henna, Golden Honey, and Persimmon; side 2: color block pattern in Natural, Rock Henna, and Natural.
Mattress 4 side 1: stripe pattern in Rose, Golden Honey, and Aqua Fog; side 2: color block pattern in Rose, Golden Honey, and Aqua Fog
Mattress 5 side 1: stripe pattern in Persimmon, Blue Thyme, and Geranium; side 2: color block pattern in Persimmon, Geranium, and Blue Thyme

stripe pattern

Rows 1 and 2: color A
Rows 3 and 4: color B
Rows 5 and 6: color C
Repeat rows 1–6 to the end.

color block pattern

Work 2 inches in each color listed; with the last color, work 2 additional rows before the bind off.

For all small mattresses, with color to start selected pattern and size 6 needles (or size needed to obtain gauge), cast on 22 stitches. Work in stockinette stitch until the side measures 6¼ inches from the cast-on edge. Bind off. Cut the yarn and pull through the remaining stitch. Steam the sides and let dry.

Cut five 6 x 3½ inch rectangles of foam.

Assemble the small mattresses as for the large mattresses.

princess
legs (make 2)

With Golden Honey, cast on 9 stitches, placing 3 stitches on each of three double-pointed needles. Join to work in the round, being careful not to twist the stitches. Place a stitch marker on the first stitch.

Round 1: knit

Round 2: (k1, m1, k1, m1, k1), repeat on each needle (5 sts per needle, 15 sts total)

Knit every round until the leg measures 3 inches from the cast-on edge. Cut the yarn and place the stitches on a stitch holder. Set aside.

For the second leg, do not cut the working yarn at the end.

Continue on to create the body:

Distribute the stitches from the 2 legs as follows:

Needle 1: 10 stitches from leg 1

Needle 2: 5 stitches from leg 1 and 5 stitches from leg 2

Needle 3: 10 stitches from leg 2

10 stitches per needle, 30 sts total.

Place a stitch marker on the first stitch on the first needle. Begin to work in the round.

Round 1: knit

Round 2: (k5, m1), repeat to end of round (12 sts per needle, 36 sts total)

Knit every round until the body measures 2 inches from the legs. With a length of yarn threaded on a yarn needle, whipstitch the hole between the legs closed. Weave the ends to the inside and trim. Stuff the legs and body with wool roving, and continue stuffing as you finish the body and head.

Decrease rounds

Round 1: (k4, k2tog), repeat to end of round (10 sts per needle, 30 sts total remain)

Round 2: knit

Round 3: (k3, k2tog), repeat to end of round (8 sts per needle, 24 sts total remain)

Round 4: knit

Round 5: (k2, k2tog), repeat to end of round (6 sts per needle, 18 sts total remain)

Round 6: knit

Round 7: (k1, k2tog), repeat to end of round (4 sts per needle, 12 sts total remain)

Rounds 8 and 9: knit

Continue on to create the head:

Round 1: (k1, m1, k2, m1, k1), repeat on each needle (6 sts per needle, 18 sts total)

Round 2: knit

Round 3: (k1, m1, k4, m1, k1), repeat on each needle (8 sts per needle, 24 sts total)

Rounds 4–9: knit

Round 10: (k2, k2tog), repeat to end of round (6 sts per needle, 18 sts total remain)

Round 11: (k1, k2tog), repeat to end of round (4 sts per needle, 12 sts total remain)

Finish stuffing the princess.

Round 12: (k2tog), repeat to end of round (2 sts per needle, 6 sts total remain)

Cut the yarn and thread on a yarn needle. Pull through the remaining stitches, gather up tight to close the hole, and stitch to secure. Weave the end to the inside and trim.

arms (make 2)

With Golden Honey, cast on 12 stitches, placing 4 stitches on each of three double-pointed needles. Join to work in the round, being careful not to twist the stitches. Place a stitch marker on the first stitch.

Knit every round until the arm measures 2½ inches from the cast-on edge.

Next round: (k2, k2tog), repeat to end of round (3 sts per needle, 9 sts total remain)

Next round: (k1, k2tog), repeat to end of round (2 sts per needle, 6 sts total remain)

Cut the yarn and thread on a yarn needle. Pull through the remaining stitches, gather up tight to close the hole, and stitch to secure. Weave the end to the inside and trim.

Stuff the arms. Thread the ends from the cast-on edges on a yarn needle and whipstitch the top of each arm closed. Whipstitch the arms to the sides of the body, using the photograph as a guide. Weave the ends to the inside and trim.

hair

With Rock Henna, cut the desired number of 12-inch lengths. Thread two lengths at a time on a yarn needle and begin pulling the lengths through individual stitches on the head of the princess. Pull through halfway until the ends meet and tie a half knot to secure. Make the hair part in the middle, then continue the part down the back of the head. Continue adding hair until you have enough pieces to make two braids. Braid the hair and tie the ends with a length of Rose. Trim the ends even.

face

With a length of black embroidery floss threaded on a yarn needle, create each eye with one long horizontal straight stitch (see p. 14), using the photograph as a guide. Catch the straight stitch with a tiny straight stitch perpendicular to the long stitch to pull it downward a bit and make the eyes look sleepy. Weave the ends through to the inside and trim. With red embroidery floss and a yarn needle, make two small straight stitches to create a mouth.

nightgown

With Rose and the larger double-pointed needles, cast on 51 stitches, leaving a long tail and arranging the stitches on the needles as follows:

Needles 1 and 2: 15 sts

Needle 3: 21 sts

Join to work in the round, being careful not to twist the stitches. Place a stitch marker on the first stitch.

Rounds 1 and 2: knit

Round 3: purl (this is the turning round)

Continue to knit every round until the nightgown measures 3 inches from the cast-on edge.

Next round: (k1, k2tog), repeat to end of round

Needles 1 and 2: 10 sts

Needle 3: 14 sts

34 stitches total remain

Next round:

Needles 1 and 2: knit

Needle 3: k2tog four times, k6 (10 sts remain)

10 sts per needle, 30 sts total remain

Continue to knit every round until the nightgown measures 4½ inches from the cast-on edge. Divide the stitches, placing 15 stitches on needle 1 and needle 3.

front

On needle 1 only, work back and forth as follows:

Row 1: knit

Row 2: purl

Row 3: k5, bind off 5 sts, k5

Turn and work on the last 5 stitches only.

Row 4: purl

Row 5: k1, ssk, k2 (4 sts remain)

Row 6: purl

Row 7: k1, ssk, k1 (3 sts remain)

Bind off. Cut the yarn and pull the end through the remaining stitch.

Reattach the yarn at the center and work on the remaining 5 stitches.

Row 1: purl

Row 2: k2, k2tog, k1 (4 sts remain)

Row 3: purl

Row 4: k1, k2tog, k1 (3 sts remain)

Bind off. Cut the yarn and pull through the remaining stitch.

back

Reattach the yarn so that you begin with a knit row. Work in stockinette stitch until the back matches the front to the shoulders, ending with a purl row. Bind off. Cut the yarn and pull through the remaining stitch.

With mattress stitch, sew the shoulders together.

crocheted edging (optional)

With Spring Green and the crochet hook, slip stitch around the neckline. Single crochet around the neckline. Slip stitch only around the armholes.

hem

Turn up the hem at the purl round and thread the tail from the cast-on stitches on a yarn needle. Whipstitch the hem to the inside. Steam the nightgown to set the hem.

embroidery

With Spring Green and a yarn needle, embroider a pea pod using straight stitches (see p. 14) and three peas using satin stitch (see p. 14) to the front of the gown. Use the photograph as a guide.

blanket

With larger needles and Celery, cast on 30 stitches. Using garter stitch, work the following stripes, carrying the Celery along the side of the blanket as you work, and cutting and weaving in the ends for the other colors.

Rows 1–8: Celery
Rows 9 and 10: Geranium
Rows 11–18: Celery
Rows 19 and 20: Aqua Fog
Rows 21–28: Celery
Rows 29 and 30: Blue Thyme
Rows 31–38: Celery
Rows 39 and 40: Natural
Rows 41–48: Celery
Rows 49 and 50: Persimmon
Rows 51–58: Celery

Bind off. Cut the yarn and pull through the remaining stitch. Weave in the ends.

crocheted edging (optional)

With Spring Green and the crochet hook, slip stitch around the edge of the blanket, working 3 stitches in each corner. Cut the yarn and pull through the remaining stitch. Weave in the end.

pea pod
pod

With Spring Green and two of the smaller double-pointed needles used as straight needles, cast on 1 stitch loosely.

Row 1: kfb until 5 stitches are on the right needle (5 sts)
Row 2: knit
Row 3: purl
Row 4: (k1, m1) four times, k1 (9 sts)
Row 5: purl
Row 6: k1, m1, k7, m1, k1 (11 sts)

Continue working in stockinette stitch until the pod measures 4 inches from the cast-on edge, ending with a purl row.

Decrease rows

Row 1: k1, ssk, k5, k2tog, k1 (7 sts remain)
Row 2: purl
Row 3: k2tog three times, k1 (4 sts remain)

Row 4: k2tog two times, do not turn, pass the first stitch over the second stitch and off of the needle (1 st remains)

vines

*With the 1 stitch remaining on the needle, use the backward-loop method to cast on 19 stitches more (20 sts).

Bind off (1 st remains).

Repeat from * two times more until there are three vines.

Repeat one more time, but cast on 29 stitches (30 sts total).

Bind off. Cut the yarn and pull the end through the remaining stitch. Weave in the ends. With a sewing needle and thread, sew one pea (see below) to the end of the longest vine.

felted wool peas (optional)

If you choose to use the felted wool balls, whip-stitch nine of them to the inside of the pod, using the sewing needle and thread. Cut two pieces of the green pipe cleaner about 3½ inches long to fit inside of the pod, running along each side of the row of peas. Secure by whipstitching the sides of the pod to the balls.

alternative to felted balls
bobbles for peas (make 9)

With the remaining Spring Green yarn, make bobbles using two smaller double-pointed needles as straight needles.

Cast on 1 stitch loosely.

Row 1: kfb until there are 5 stitches on the right needle (5 sts)
Row 2: knit
Row 3: purl
Row 4: knit, do not turn, pass the second, third, and fourth stitches over the first stitch and off the needle

Cut the yarn and pull through the remaining stitch.

Thread the tail on a yarn needle and gather up the edges with a few stitches to create a ball. Finish as for the felted wool balls.

christmas set

I wanted to include one holiday toy in the collection, and this Santa set is it. Knitters love creating special pieces for Christmas and many do it all year round. Cast on for this in time to have it done by December, then watch the smiles when you bring it out!

This Santa is beautifully crafted, with wonderful detail, and the kids can play with him all they want; he can't break. The gift bag is a cute addition, ideal for tossing around or for imagining what might be inside. The tiny Christmas mouse is the tag-along seasonal friend, the perfect stocking stuffer. If you add a loop on top, he can even be an ornament for the tree.

You can't go wrong investing in this sweet set that will be cherished and enjoyed for many years to come. Ho, ho, ho!

finished measurements

- Santa: 8 inches tall, including the hat; 5 inches wide
- Bag: 4 inches tall, 4 inches wide
- Christmas mouse: 3 inches tall, 2 inches wide

yarn

- Rowan Handknit Cotton (100% cotton; 93 yards/50 grams), 1 skein each in Rosso #215, Black #252, Gooseberry #219, Shell #310, and Bleached #263

tools

- U.S. size 3 set of four double-pointed needles, or size needed to obtain gauge
- Tape measure or ruler
- Scissors
- Yarn needle
- Stitch markers
- Polyester fiberfill, 1 small bag
- Poly pellets (optional), 32-ounce bag

gauge

- 6 stitches per inch in stockinette stitch

santa

body

Starting at the bottom, with Rosso, cast on 9 stitches, placing 3 stitches on each of three double-pointed needles. Join to work in the round, being careful not to twist the stitches. Place a stitch marker on the first stitch.

Increase round: (kfb, k to last stitch, kfb), repeat on each needle (5 sts per needle, 15 sts total)

Repeat the increase round until there are 25 stitches on each needle, 75 stitches total.

Next round: purl

Knit every round until the body measures ¾ inch from the purl row.

Switch to Bleached.

Knit 2 rounds.

Switch to Rosso.

Knit every round until the body measures 3 inches from the purl round.

Decrease rounds

Round 1: (k3, k2tog), repeat to end of round (20 sts per needle, 60 sts total remain)

Round 2: (k2, k2tog), repeat to end of round (15 sts per needle, 45 sts total remain)

Round 3: (k1, k2tog), repeat to end of round (10 sts per needle, 30 sts total remain)

Thread the tail from the cast-on stitches on a yarn needle. Stitch through all of the cast-on stitches, gather up to close the hole at the bottom, and stitch to secure. Weave the end to the inside and trim. Fill the body half full with poly pellets and the rest with fiberfill, or stuff with fiberfill only.

Round 4: k2tog, repeat to end of round (5 sts per needle, 15 sts total remain)

Round 5: (k2tog, k1, k2tog), repeat on each needle (3 sts per needle, 9 sts total remain)

Finish stuffing.

Cut the yarn and thread the end on a yarn needle. Pull the end through the remaining stitches, gather up tight to close the hole, and stitch to secure. Weave the end to the inside and trim.

head

Starting at the bottom of the head with Shell, cast on 9 stitches, placing 3 stitches on each of three double-pointed needles. Join to work in the round, being careful not to twist the stitches. Place a stitch marker on the first stitch.

Round 1: kfb in every stitch (6 sts per needle, 18 sts total)

Round 2: (k1, kfb), repeat to end of round (9 sts per needle, 27 sts total)

Round 3: (k2, kfb), repeat to end of round (12 sts per needle, 36 sts total)

Rounds 4–15: knit

Decrease rounds

Round 16: (k2, k2tog), repeat to end of round (9 sts per needle, 27 sts total remain)

Thread the tail from the cast-on stitches on a yarn needle. Stitch through all the cast-on stitches, gather tightly to close the hole, and stitch to secure. Stuff the head with fiberfill.

Round 17: (k1, k2tog), repeat to end of round (6 sts per needle, 18 sts total remain)

Round 18: k2tog, repeat to end of round (3 sts per needle, 9 sts total remain)

Finish stuffing.

Cut the yarn and thread the tail on a yarn needle. Pull through the remaining stitches, gather up tight to close the hole, and stitch to secure. Use this tail and the yarn needle to whip-stitch the head to the body. Weave the end to the inside and trim.

hat

With Bleached, cast on 36 stitches, placing 12 stitches on each of three double-pointed needles. Join to work in the round, being careful not to twist the stitches. Place a stitch marker on the first stitch.

Rounds 1–3: knit

Switch to Rosso.

Rounds 4–6: knit

Switch to Bleached.

Round 7: knit

Repeat rounds 4 through 7 until the hat measures 1½ inches from the cast-on edge.

Decrease rounds

Continue in Rosso only.

Round 1: (k2, k2tog), repeat to end of round (9 sts per needle, 27 sts total remain)

Rounds 2–4: knit

Round 5: (k1, k2tog), repeat to end of round (6 sts per needle, 18 sts total remain)

Rounds 6–11: knit

Round 12: (k2tog), repeat to end of round (3 sts per needle, 9 sts total remain)

Rounds 13–17: knit

Cut the yarn and thread the tail on a yarn needle. Pull the end through the remaining stitches, gather up tight to close the hole, and stitch to secure. Weave the end to the inside and trim.

Make one bobble with Bleached as follows:

Using two double-pointed needles as straight needles, cast on 1 stitch loosely.

Row 1: kfb until there are 3 stitches on the right needle (3 sts)

Row 2: knit

Row 3: purl

Row 4: knit, do not turn, pass the first, second, and third stitches over the first stitch and off the needle

Cut the yarn and thread the tail on a yarn needle. Take a few stitches around the edge of the bobble, and gather the stitches to create a ball. Attach the bobble on the top of the hat with a few stitches. Weave the end to the inside and trim. Thread the tail from the cast-on edge on a yarn needle. Place the hat on the head and whipstitch to attach. Weave the end to the inside and trim.

beard

With Bleached and two double-pointed needles used as straight needles, cast on 3 stitches.

Row 1: kfb, k1, kfb (5 sts)

Row 2: purl

Row 3: kfb, k3, kfb (7 sts)

Row 4: purl

Row 5: kfb, k5, kfb (9 sts)

Row 6: purl

Row 7: knit

Row 8: purl

Row 9: knit to end, cast on 8 stitches (17 sts)

Row 10: purl to end, cast on 8 stitches (25 sts)

Row 11: knit

Row 12: purl

Bind off. Cut the yarn and pull through the remaining stitch. Cut an 18-inch length of Bleached and thread on a yarn needle. Starting at the top of the beard, complete four rows of satin stitch (see p. 14). Whipstitch the top edge of the beard to the face.

face

Using the photograph as a guide, with a length of Rosso threaded on a yarn needle make one French knot (see p. 15) for the nose. With Black and a yarn needle, take 2 straight stitches (see p. 14) for the eyes. With Bleached, take 2 straight stitches and wrap the yarn (see p. 15) 4 times over the straight stitches for the eyebrows. For the mustache, take 2 straight stitches under the nose and above the beard, and wrap 4 times on each set of 2 straight stitches.

arms (make 2)

With Rosso, cast on 12 stitches, placing 4 stitches on each of three double-pointed needles. Join to work in the round, being careful not to twist the stitches. Place a stitch marker on the first stitch.

Knit every round until the arm measures 1½ inches from the cast-on edge.

Switch to Bleached.

Knit 3 rounds.

Bind off. Cut the yarn, leaving a long tail, and thread on a yarn needle. Pull through the remaining stitch. Using the yarn needle, whipstitch decoratively around the White rounds at the bottom of the arm. Weave in the end and trim.

hands (make 2)

With Black, cast on 9 stitches, placing 3 stitches on each of three double-pointed needles. Join to work in the round, being careful not to twist the stitches. Place a stitch marker on the first stitch.

Round 1: knit

Round 2: (kfb, k2), repeat on each needle (4 sts per needle, 12 sts total)

Rounds 3–8: knit

Bind off. Cut the yarn and pull the end through the remaining stitch. Thread the tail from the cast-on edge on a yarn needle, stitch through all of the cast-on stitches, gather up tight to close the hole, and stitch to secure. Fill the hand with poly pellets or fiberfill. Thread the end from the bound-off stitches on a yarn needle and whipstitch the top of the hand closed. Whipstitch the hand to the cuff of the arm.

thumbs (make 2)

With Black and 2 double-pointed needles used as straight needles, cast on 2 stitches. Work in I-cord (see p. 00) for 4 rows.

Next row: k2tog (1 st remains)

Cut the yarn and pull through the remaining stitch. With a couple of whipstitches, attach the thumb to the side of the hand, thumb facing forward.

legs (make 2)

With Rosso, cast on 9 stitches, placing 3 stitches on each of three double-pointed needles. Join to work in the round, being careful not to twist the stitches. Place a stitch marker on the first stitch.

Knit every round until the leg measures 1 inch from the cast-on edge.

Bind off. Cut the yarn and pull through the remaining stitch. Thread the end on a yarn needle and whipstitch along the cast-on stitches so that one half of the stitches lies flat against the other. Repeat for the bound-off end.

feet (make 2)

With Black, cast on 9 stitches, placing 3 stitches on each of three double-pointed needles. Join to work in the round, being careful not to twist the stitches. Place a stitch marker on the first stitch.

Round 1: knit

Round 2: (kfb, k2), repeat on each needle (4 sts per needle, 12 sts total)

Rounds 3–10: knit

Round 11: (ssk, k2), repeat on each needle (3 sts per needle, 9 sts total remain)

Thread the tail from the cast-on edge on a yarn needle, stitch through all of the cast-on stitches, and gather up tight close the hole. Stitch to secure. Weave the end to the inside and trim.

Fill the feet with poly pellets or stuff with fiberfill. Cut the yarn and thread the tail on a yarn needle. Pull through the remaining stitches and gather up to close the hole. Whipstitch the top of the feet to the legs. With a length of Rosso threaded on a yarn needle, whipstitch the legs to the bottom side of the body, setting the legs back

a couple of rows from the purl row. Weave the ends to the inside and trim.

santa's bag

With Gooseberry, cast on 9 stitches, placing 3 stitches on each of three double-pointed needles. Join to work in the round, being careful not to twist the stitches. Place a stitch marker on the first stitch.

Round 1: knit

Round 2: kfb in every stitch (6 stitches per needle, 18 stitches total)

Round 3: (k1, kfb), repeat to end of round (9 sts per needle, 27 sts total)

Round 4: (k2, kfb), repeat to end of round (12 sts per needle, 36 sts total)

Round 5: (k3, kfb), repeat to end of round (15 sts per needle, 45 sts total)

Round 6: (k4, kfb), repeat to end of round (18 sts per needle, 54 sts total)

Round 7: (k5, kfb), repeat to end of round (21 sts per needle, 63 sts total)

Place a stitch marker on round 7 and leave it there.

Knit every round until bag measures 3 inches from the stitch marker.

Decrease rounds

Round 1: (k5, k2tog), repeat to end of round (18 sts per needle, 54 sts total remain)

Round 2: (k4, k2tog), repeat to end of round (15 sts per needle, 45 sts total remain)

Rounds 3–4: knit

Round 5: (k3, k2tog), repeat to end of round (12 sts per needle, 36 sts total remain)

Round 6: knit

Round 7: (k2, k2tog), repeat to end of round (9 sts per needle, 27 sts total remain)

Round 8: knit

Thread the tail from the cast-on edge on a yarn needle, stitch through all of the cast-on stitches, and gather up to close the hole at the bottom. Stitch to secure. Fill the bag one-third full with poly pellets and the rest with fiberfill, or stuff with fiberfill only.

Round 9: (k1, k2tog), repeat to end of round (6 sts per needle, 18 sts total remain)

Rounds 10–15: knit

Round 16: kfb in every stitch (12 sts per needle, 36 sts total remain)

Rounds 17 and 18: knit

Bind off in k1, p1 rib. Cut the yarn and pull through the remaining stitch. Weave the end into the inside of the bag and trim so end stays inside.

tie

With Rosso and two double-pointed needles used as straight needles, cast on 2 stitches. Work in I-cord until the tie measures 8 inches from the cast-on edge.

Next row: k2tog (1 st remains)

Cut the yarn and pull through the remaining stitch. Weave the ends to the inside.

Make 2 bobbles with Bleached as for the top of the hat. Whipstitch one bobble to each end of the tie, weave in ends, and trim.

christmas mouse
body

With Bleached, cast on 9 stitches, placing 3 stitches on each of three double-pointed needles. Join to work in the round, being careful not to twist the stitches. Place a stitch marker on the first stitch.

Round 1: knit

Round 2: (kfb, k1, kfb), repeat on each needle (5 sts per needle, 15 stitches total)

Round 3: knit

Round 4: (kfb, k3, kfb), repeat on each needle (7 sts per needle, 21 sts total)

Round 5: (kfb, k5, kfb), repeat on each needle (9 sts per needle, 27 sts total)

Rounds 6–12: knit

Decrease rounds

Round 13: (ssk, k5, k2tog), repeat on each needle (7 sts per needle, 21 sts total remain)

Round 14: (ssk, k3, k2tog), repeat on each needle (5 sts per needle, 15 sts total remain)

Thread the tail from the cast-on edge on a yarn needle. Stitch through all of the cast-on stitches, gather tight to close the hole at the bottom, and stitch to secure. Stuff the body with fiberfill.

Round 15: (ssk, k1, k2tog), repeat on each needle (3 sts per needle, 9 sts total remain)

Cut the yarn and thread the tail on a yarn needle. Pull through the remaining stitches, gather up tight to close the hole, and stitch to secure. Weave the end to the inside and trim.

head

Complete the same as for the body through round 4 (7 sts per needle, 21 stitches total).

Rounds 5–9: knit

Decrease rounds for nose

Round 10: (ssk, k3, k2tog), repeat on each needle (5 sts per needle, 15 stitches total remain)

Rounds 11 and 12: knit

Round 13: (ssk, k1, k2tog), repeat on each needle (3 sts per needle, 9 stitches total remain)

Rounds 14 and 15: knit

Thread the tail from the cast-on edge on a yarn needle. Stitch through all of the cast-on stitches, pull up tight to close the hole, and stitch to secure. Weave the end to the inside and trim. Stuff with fiberfill. Cut the yarn, and thread on a yarn needle. Pull the end through the remaining stitches, gather tight to close the hole, and stitch to secure. Weave the end to the inside and trim.

outer ears (make 2)

With Bleached and two double-pointed needles used as straight needles, cast on 5 stitches.

Row 1: knit

Row 2: pfb, p3, pfb (7 sts)

Row 3: knit

Row 4: purl

Row 5: knit

Row 6: purl

Row 7: ssk, k3, k2tog (5 sts remain)
Row 8: p2tog, p1, p2tog (3 sts remain)

Bind off. Cut the yarn and pull through the remaining stitch.

inner ears (make 2)

With Gooseberry and 2 double-pointed needles used as straight needles, cast on 3 stitches.
Row 1: knit
Row 2: pfb, p1, pfb (5 sts)
Row 3: knit
Row 4: purl
Row 5: ssk, k1, k2tog (3 sts remain)

Bind off. Cut the yarn and pull through the remaining stitch. Place one inner ear piece on each outer ear piece, purl sides facing, and with the tail from the outer ear threaded on a yarn needle, whipstitch around the edges of each ear. With a length of Bleached threaded on a yarn needle, whipstitch the ears to the head, using the photograph as a guide. Whipstitch the head to the body, weave the ends to the inside, and trim.

nose

With Rosso and two double-pointed needles used as straight needles, cast on 1 stitch loosely.
Row 1: kfb (2 stitches)
Row 2: knit

Do not turn. Pull the first stitch over the second stitch and off the needle. Cut the yarn and pull through the remaining stitch. Thread the end on a yarn needle, stitch around the edge of the piece, and gather the stitches to form a ball. Whipstitch the nose to the tip of the snout.

tail

With Bleached and two double-pointed needles used as straight needles, cast on 2 stitches. Work in I-cord until the piece measures 3 inches from the cast-on edge.
Next row: k2tog (1 st remains)

Cut the yarn and pull through the remaining stitch. Thread the end on a yarn needle, weave

it into the tail, and trim. Thread the tail from the cast-on stitches on a yarn needle and whipstitch to the lower back center of the body, using the photograph as a guide. Weave the end to the inside and trim.

legs and arms (make 4 total)

With Bleached and two double-pointed needles used as straight needles, cast on 3 stitches. Work in I-cord until the piece measures 1 inch, and bind off.

Cut the yarn and thread the tail on a yarn needle. Whipstitch the arms to the sides of the body and the legs to the lower front of the body. Weave in the remaining ends.

feet and hands (make 4 total)

With Bleached and two double-pointed needles used as straight needles, cast on 1 stitch loosely.
Row 1: kfb until there are 3 stitches on the right needle
Row 2: knit
Row 3: purl
Row 4: knit, do not turn, pass the first, second, and third stitches over the first stitch and off the needle (1 stitch remains)

Cut the yarn, thread on a yarn needle, and stitch around the edge of the piece. Gather the stitches to form a ball, and whipstitch one bobble to the end of each arm and leg. Weave all ends to the inside and trim.

scarf

With Rosso and two double-pointed needles used as straight needles, cast on 3 stitches. Knit every row until the scarf measures 7 inches.

Bind off. Cut the yarn and pull through the remaining stitch.

With Gooseberry, make two 1-inch pom-poms with 10 wraps each. With a yarn needle and the ends, attach one pom-pom to each end of the scarf. Tie the scarf around the mouse's neck.

matryoshka

If you look around the crafting world, you will see Russian nesting dolls everywhere you turn. The cute characters, often wrapped up in babushkas, are printed on fabric, crocheted, felted, and painted. I even have a set of matryoshka salt and pepper shakers. The only kind of set I'd never seen was a functional knitted one that you could actually play with. I knew what I had to do, and set out to come up with the features of the design.

I kept my knitted set of dolls small so that the repetitive format remains interesting, and kept them all one color to keep things simple. The doll set takes a small amount of worsted-weight yarn, less than one skein, and is the perfect stash buster. With a little simple embroidery for the faces, you are all set to nest.

These dolls are a bit addictive; you may have to make more than one set!

finished measurements

- Large doll: 4½ inches tall
- Medium doll: 4 inches tall
- Small doll: 3½ inches tall
- Tiny doll: 1½ inches tall

yarn

- Blue Sky Dyed Cotton (100% organically grown cotton; 150 yards/100 grams), 1 skein in Aloe #604
- Blue Sky Skinny Organic (100% organic cotton; 150 yards/65 grams), 1 skein in Birch #30

tools

- U.S. size 3 set of four double-pointed needles, or size needed to obtain gauge
- Stitch marker
- Tape measure
- Scissors
- Yarn needle
- Embroidery floss in yellow, pink, red, and black
- Embroidery needle
- Small amount of fiberfill

gauge

- 6 stitches per inch in stockinette stitch

large doll

bottom

With Aloe, cast on 9 stitches, placing 3 stitches on each of three double-pointed needles. Join to work in the round, being careful not to twist the stitches. Place a stitch marker on the first stitch of the round.

Round 1: knit

Round 2: kfb in each stitch (6 sts on each needle, 9 sts total)

Rounds 3–5: knit

Round 6: kfb in each stitch (12 sts on each needle, 36 sts total)

Round 7: knit

Round 8: purl

Rounds 9 and 10: knit

Round 11: (k2, kfb in the next stitch), repeat across the round (16 sts per needle, 48 sts total)

Continue, knitting every round until the bottom measures 1½ inches from the purl round.

Purl 2 rounds.

Knit 3 rounds.

Bind off.

Cut the yarn, leaving a 6-inch-long tail. Turn the bottom inside out so the purl side is facing out. Using the two consecutive purl rounds as the turning rows, fold the hem to the purl side of the bottom. Using a yarn needle and a length of Aloe, whipstitch the bound-off edge to the purl side of the bottom. Turn the bottom right side out so the knit side is facing out. Stitch up the hole in the cast-on edge and weave the ends to the inside.

top

With Aloe, cast on 48 stitches, placing 16 stitches on each of three double-pointed needles. Join to work in the round, being careful not to twist the stitches. Place a stitch marker on the first stitch of the round.

Knit 3 rounds.

Purl 2 rounds.

Continue, knitting every round until the top measures 1¼ inches from the purl rounds.

Next round: (k2, k2tog), repeat across the round (12 sts per needle, 36 sts total remain)

Next round: (k1, ssk, k6, k2tog, k1), repeat on each needle (10 sts per needle, 30 sts total remain)

Place a stitch marker on this round.

Knit straight until the top measures 1¼ inches from the marker.

Decrease rounds

Round 1: (k3, k2tog), repeat across the round (8 sts per needle, 24 sts total remain)

Round 2: (k2, k2tog), repeat across the round (6 sts per needle, 18 sts total remain)

Round 3: (k1, k2tog), repeat across the round (4 sts per needle, 12 sts total remain)

Round 4: (k2tog), repeat across the round (2 sts per needle, 6 sts total remain)

Cut the yarn, leaving a 4-inch-long tail. Pull the tail through the remaining stitches, gather up tight to close the hole, and stitch to secure. Weave the tail to the inside and trim. Using the purl rows as the turning row, fold the hem under to the inside. Using the cast-on tail threaded on a yarn needle, whipstitch the hem to the purl side of the top. (It is easier to sew down if the top is turned inside out while sewing.) Weave in all ends.

face

With Birch and two double-pointed needles used as straight needles, cast on 3 stitches.

Row 1: kfb, k1, kfb (5 sts)

Row 2: pfb, p3, pfb (7 sts)

Row 3: kfb, k5, kfb (9 sts)

Rows 4–8: start with a purl row and begin to work in stockinette stitch (knit 1 row, purl 1 row)

Row 9: ssk, k5, k2tog (7 sts remain)

Row 10: p2tog, p3, p2tog (5 sts remain)

Row 11: ssk, k1, k2tog (3 sts remain)

Bind off in purl.

Cut the yarn, leaving a 6-inch-long tail, and pull through the last stitch.

Embroider the face with the embroidery needle and floss, using the photograph as a guide. The cheeks are made with spiderweb circles (see p. 13). The mouth and hair are made with satin stitches. The nose and eyes are straight stitches.

Thread the tail from the bind-off edge of the face on the yarn needle. Whipstitch the embroidered face piece to the front top of the doll.

medium doll

bottom

With Aloe, cast on 9 stitches, placing 3 stitches on each of three double-pointed needles. Join to work in the round, being careful not to twist the stitches. Place a stitch marker on the first stitch.

Round 1: knit

Round 2: kfb in each stitch (6 sts per needle, 18 sts total)

Rounds 3 and 4: knit

Round 5: (k1, kfb) across the round (9 sts per needle, 27 sts total)

Round 6: purl

Rounds 7 and 8: knit

Round 9: (k2, kfb) across the round (12 sts per needle, 36 sts total)

Continue, knitting every round until the bottom measures 1 inch from the purl round.

Purl 2 rounds.

Knit 3 rounds.

Bind off. Finish as for the large bottom.

top

With Aloe, cast on 36 stitches, placing 12 stitches on each of three double-pointed needles. Join to work in the round, being careful not to twist the stitches. Place a marker on the first stitch of the round.

Knit 3 rounds.

Purl 2 rounds.

Knit every round until the top measures 1 inch from the purl rounds.

Next round: (k2, k2tog), repeat across the round (9 sts per needle, 27 sts total remain)

Next round: (k1, ssk, k3, k2tog, k1), repeat on each needle (7 sts per needle, 21 sts total)

Place a stitch marker on this round.

Knit every round until the top measures ¾ inch from the stitch marker.

Decrease rounds

Round 1: (k5, k2tog), repeat across the round (6 sts per needle, 18 sts total remain)

Round 2: (k4, k2tog), repeat across the round (5 sts per needle, 15 sts total remain)

Round 3: (k3, k2tog), repeat across the round (4 sts per needle, 12 sts total remain)

Round 4: (k2, k2tog), repeat across the round (3 sts per needle, 9 sts total remain)

Round 5: (k1, k2tog), repeat across the round (2 sts per needle, 6 sts total remain)

Cut the yarn, leaving a 4-inch-long tail, and thread on the yarn needle. Pull through the remaining stitches, gather up tight, and stitch to secure. Weave the end to the inside.

face

With Birch and two double-pointed needles used as straight needles, cast on 3 stitches.

Row 1: kfb, k1, kfb (5 sts)

Row 2: pfb, p3, pfb (7 sts)

Rows 3–7: start with a knit row and continue working in stockinette stitch

Row 8: ssk, k3, k2tog (5 sts remain)

Row 9: p2tog, p1, p2tog (3 sts)

Bind off. Cut the yarn, leaving a 6-inch-long tail, and pull through the remaining stitch.

Embroider the face with the embroidery needle and floss, using the photograph as a guide, same as the large doll.

Thread the tail from the bind-off edge of the face on a yarn needle and whipstitch the face to the top. Weave the ends to the inside.

small doll
bottom

With Aloe, cast on 9 stitches, placing 3 stitches on each of three double-pointed needles. Join to work in the round, being careful not to twist the stitches. Place a marker on the first stitch.

Round 1: knit

Round 2: kfb in each stitch (6 sts per needle, 18 stitches total)

Round 3: knit

Round 4: purl

Round 5: knit

Round 6: (k1, kfb), repeat across the round (9 sts per needle, 27 sts total remain)

Continue knitting every round until the bottom measures ¾ inch from the purl round.

Purl 2 rounds.

Knit 3 rounds.

Bind off. Finish as for the large bottom.

top

With Aloe, cast on 27 stitches, placing 9 stitches on each of three double-pointed needles. Join to work in the round, being careful not to twist the stitches. Place a stitch marker on the first stitch of the round.

Knit 3 rounds.

Purl 2 rounds.

Continue, knitting every round until the top measures ¾ inch from the purl rounds.

Decrease rounds
Round 1: (ssk, k5, k2 tog), repeat across the round (7 sts per needle, 21 sts total remain)
Round 2: (ssk, k3, k2tog), repeat across the round (5 sts per needle, 15 sts total remain)

Place a stitch marker on this round. Knit every round until the top measures ½ inch from the purl rounds.
Next round: (ssk, k1, k2tog), repeat across the round (3 sts per needle, 9 sts total)

Cut the yarn and thread the tail on a yarn needle. Pull through the remaining stitches, pull up tight to close the hole, and stitch to secure. Weave the end to the inside and trim.

face
With Birch and two double-pointed needles used as straight needles, cast on 3 stitches.
Row 1: kfb, k1, kfb (5 sts)
Row 2: purl
Row 3: knit
Row 4: purl
Row 5: ssk, k1, k2tog (3 sts remain)

Bind off. Cut the yarn, leaving a 4-inch-long tail.

Embroider the face with the embroidery needle and floss, using the phtograph as a guide. For the small face, use straight stitches for the cheeks. The rest is the same as for the large face.

Thread the tail from the bind-off edge of the face on a yarn needle and whipstitch the face to the top. Weave the ends to the inside.

tiny doll
With Aloe, cast on 9 stitches, placing 3 stitches on each of three double-pointed needles.
Round 1: knit
Round 2: purl
Rounds 3 and 4: knit
Round 5: (k1, kfb, k1), repeat across the round (4 sts per needle, 12 sts total)

Continue, knitting every round until doll measures ½ inch from the purl round.
Next round: (k1, k2tog, k1), repeat across the round (3 sts per needle, 9 sts total remain)

Knit 2 rounds. Stuff the doll with fiberfill.
Next round: (k1, k2tog), repeat across the round (2 sts per needle, 6 sts total remain)

Cut the yarn and thread on a yarn needle. Pull through the remaining stitches, pull up tight, and stitch to secure. Weave the end to the inside and trim.

face
With Birch and two double-pointed needles used as straight needles, cast on 1 stitch.
Row 1: knit into the front, back, then front again (3 sts)
Row 2: purl
Row 3: knit
Row 4: purl
Row 5: knit, do not turn, pass the second and third stitches over the first stitch and off the needle (1 st remains)

Cut the yarn, leaving a 4-inch-long tail, and pull it through the remaining stitch.

Embroider the face with the embroidery needle and floss, using tiny straight stitches for hair, eyes, mouth, and cheeks.

Thread the tail from the bind-off edge of the face on a yarn needle and whipstitch the face to the top. Weave the ends to the inside.

baby doll set

My younger daughter is a baby doll aficionado. She enjoys a good play session with her collection, which contains every sort of doll imaginable, each with its own personality and purpose. She inspired me to knit up the perfect baby doll set—and helped me with the design.

The size is perfect for cuddling, as the doll fits right in the crook of a child's arm; it's not too big or too small. Her hair is no-fuss and fun to make. Plus she can either sit or lie down.

I used the most fantastic organic cotton yarn to keep the doll extra special. The construction is simple, with minimal seaming at the end. The legs have a knee bend worked in, which is fun to knit. My daughter insisted on the sundress, ruffle pants, and hat. She also requested the matching hat for the baby's mom, too!

finished measurements

- Baby doll: 9 inches tall seated, 5 inches wide
- Child's hat: To fit 2 years and older, head circumference of 18–20 inches

yarn

- Baby doll: Rowan Purelife Organic Cotton (100% naturally dyed organic cotton; 131 yards/50 grams), 2 skeins in Quebracho Bark #987
- Sundress, baby doll's hat with braids, and baby doll's hair: 1 skein each in Madder #980, Lipstick Tree #985, and Yellowwood #984
- Ruffle pants: 1 skein in Natural #986
- Child's hat: 1 skein in Madder #980, small amount of Lipstick Tree #985 for loop, and small amount of Yellowwood #984 for braids

tools

- U.S. size 4 set of four double-pointed needles and 24-inch circular or straight needles (used for baby doll and ruffle pants), or size needed to obtain gauge
- U.S. size 5 set of four double-pointed needles, 12-inch circular needle (used for baby doll's hat), and 16-inch circular needle (used for sundress and child's hat), or size needed to obtain gauge
- U.S. size G crochet hook (optional)
- Tape measure or ruler
- Scissors
- Stitch markers
- Yarn needle
- Polyester fiberfill, 1 small bag
- Poly pellets (optional), 32-ounce bag
- Brown and white embroidery floss
- Embroidery needle

gauge

- 6 stitches per inch in stockinette stitch for baby doll
- 5½ stitches per inch in stockinette stitch for baby doll's hat, girl's hat, and sundress

baby doll

body

With Quebracho Bark, cast on 9 stitches, placing 3 stitches on each of three of the smaller double-pointed needles. Join to work in the round, being careful not to twist the stitches. Place a stitch marker on the first stitch.

Increase rounds
Round 1: knit
Round 2: kfb in every stitch (6 sts per needle, 18 sts total)
Rounds 3–5: knit
Round 6: kfb in every stitch (12 sts per needle, 36 sts total)

Rounds 7–9: knit

Round 10: (k2, kfb), repeat to end of round
(16 sts per needle, 48 sts total)

Round 11: knit

Round 12: (k3, kfb), repeat to end of round
(20 sts per needle, 60 sts total)

Rounds 13–15: knit

Round 16: (k4, kfb), repeat to end of round
(24 sts per needle, 72 sts total)

Place a stitch marker on round 16 and leave it there. Knit every round until the body measures 3 inches from the stitch marker.

Decrease rounds

Round 1: (k4, k2tog), repeat to end of round
(20 sts per needle, 60 sts total remain)

Rounds 2–5: knit

Thread the tail from the cast-on stitches on a yarn needle. Stitch through all of the stitches in the cast-on edge, gather to close the hole at the bottom, and stitch to secure (see p. 16). Weave the end to the inside and trim.

Fill the body one-third full with poly pellets and the rest with fiberfill, or fill with fiberfill only. Continue to add stuffing as you work on the body.

Round 6: (k3, k2tog), repeat to end of round
(16 sts per needle, 48 sts total remain)

Rounds 7–9: knit

Round 10: (k2, k2tog), repeat to end of round
(12 sts per needle, 36 sts total remain)

Rounds 11–13: knit

Round 14: (k1, k2tog), repeat to end of round
(8 sts per needle, 24 sts total remain)

Round 15: knit

Round 16: (k2, k2tog) repeat to end of round
(4 sts per needle, 12 sts total remain)

Round 17: knit

Round 18: (k1, k2tog, k1), repeat to end of round
(3 sts per needle, 9 sts total remain)

Finish stuffing. Cut the yarn and thread the end on a yarn needle. Pull through the remaining stitches, gather up tight to close the hole, and stitch to secure. Weave the end to the inside and trim.

head

Starrting at the bottom of the head, work the same as for the body through round 16 of the increase rounds (24 sts per needle, 72 sts total).

Place a stitch marker on round 16 and leave it there. Knit every round until the head measures 3½ inches from the stitch marker.

Decrease rounds (for the top of the head)

Round 1: (k4, k2tog), repeat to end of round
(20 sts per needle, 60 sts total remain)

Round 2: knit

Round 3: (k3, k2tog), repeat to end of round
(16 sts per needle, 48 sts total remain)

Rounds 4 and 5: knit

Round 6: (k2, k2tog), repeat to end of round
(12 sts per needle, 36 sts total remain)

Round 7: knit

Round 8: (k1, k2tog), repeat to end of round
(8 sts per needle, 24 sts total remain)

Round 9: knit

Thread the tail from the cast-on stitches on a yarn needle. Stitch through all of the stitches in the cast-on edge, gather to close the hole at the bottom, and stitch to secure. Weave the end to the inside and trim. Stuff the head with fiberfill. Continue to stuff as you work.

Round 10: k2tog, repeat to end of round
(4 sts per needle, 12 sts total remain)

Round 11: (k1, k2tog, k1), repeat to end of round
(3 sts per needle, 9 sts total remain)

Finish stuffing. Cut the yarn, leaving a 6-inch-long tail, and thread on a yarn needle. Pull the end through the remaining stitches, pull up tight to close the hole, and stitch to secure. Use the remainder of the tail to whipstitch the head to the body.

ears (make 2)

With Quebracho Bark, cast on 12 stitches, leaving an 8-inch-long tail, and placing 4 stitches on each of three double-pointed needles. Join to work in the round, being careful not to twist the stitches. Place a stitch marker on the first stitch.

Rounds 1 and 2: knit

Round 3: (k2, k2tog), repeat to end of round
(3 sts per needle, 9 sts total remain)

Cut the yarn and thread the end on a yarn needle. Pull the end through the remaining stitches, up tight to close the hole, and stitch to secure. Weave the end to the inside and trim. Lay the ear flat and whipstitch the cast-on edge closed, using the tail threaded on a yarn needle. With the remainder of the cast-on tail, whipstitch the ears to the side of the head, using the photograph as a guide.

hair (make 3 pieces)

With Yellowwood and two double-pointed needles used as straight needles, cast on 6 stitches.

Row 1: work twisted loop stitch in every stitch as follows:

Knit the stitch and leave it on the left needle.

Pull the loop that is on the right needle out about 3 inches. Transfer the loop onto your right index finger. Twist the loop in one direction until it folds back on itself.

Place the loop back on the left needle.

Knit the two stitches together.

Row 2: knit

Row 3: repeat row 1

Bind off. Cut the yarn and pull through the remaining stitch. Arrange the hair pieces on the top of the head in a cluster. Using the tails threaded on a yarn needle, whipstitch the hair down. Weave the ends to the inside and trim.

arms (make 2)

Starting at the shoulder, with Quebracho Bark and two double-pointed needles used as straight needles, cast on 5 stitches, leaving an 8-inch-long tail.

Row 1: kfb, k to last stitch, kfb (7 sts)

Row 2: purl

Repeat rows 1 and 2 until there are 15 stitches, ending with a purl row.

Next row: kfb, k6, kfb, k6, kfb (18 sts)

Place 6 stitches on each of three double-pointed needles. Continue working in the round. Place a stitch marker on the first stitch and leave it there. Knit every round until the arm measures 2¼ inches from the stitch marker.

Continue on to create the wrist and hand:

Round 1: (k4, k2tog), repeat to end of round (5 sts per needle, 15 sts total remain)

Round 2: knit

Round 3: (kfb, k3, kfb), on each needle (7 sts per needle, 21 sts total)

Rounds 4–10: knit

Round 11: k to last 2 sts, k2tog (20 sts total remain)

Rearrange the stitches, placing 10 stitches on each of two double-pointed needles.

Continue working in the round as follows:

Round 12: (ssk, k6, k2tog), on each needle (8 sts per needle, 16 sts total remain)

Round 13: knit

Round 14: (ssk, k4, k2tog), on each needle (6 sts per needle, 12 sts total remain)

Cut the yarn, leaving an 8-inch-long tail. Thread the end on a yarn needle.

Use kitchener stitch (see p. 9) to graft the tip of the hand.

Fill the hand with poly pellets and stuff the arm lightly with fiberfill, or stuff both with fiberfill only. Pinch the shoulder end of the arm flat and whipstitch the edges shut, using the tail from the cast-on edge. With the remaining length of the cast-on tail, whipstitch the arms to the body. The slanting shoulder should follow the curve of the body.

thumbs (make 2)

With Quebracho Bark, cast on 6 stitches, placing 2 stitches on each of three double-pointed needles. Join to work in the round, being careful not to twist the stitches. Place a stitch marker on the first stitch.

Knit 3 rounds.

Cut the yarn and thread the end on a yarn needle. Pull through the stitches, pull up tight to close, and stitch to secure. Stuff lightly with fiberfill. Thread the tail from the cast-on edge on a yarn needle and whipstitch the thumb to the side of the hand, facing upward. Weave the end to the inside and trim.

legs (make 2)

With Quebracho Bark, cast on 24 stitches, placing 8 stitches on each of three double-pointed needles. Join to work in the round, being careful not to twist the stitches. Place a stitch marker on the first stitch.

Knit every round until the leg measures 2 inches from the cast-on edge.

Rearrange the stitches to work the knee bend as follows:

Needle 1: 18 sts
Needle 2: 3 sts
Needle 3: 3 sts

Switch to working back and forth on needle 1 only as follows:

Row 1: k11, k2tog, k1, turn
Row 2: sl1, p5, p2tog, p1, turn
Row 3: sl1, k6, k2tog, k1, turn
Row 4: sl1, p7, p2tog, p1, turn
Row 5: sl1, k8, k2tog, k1, turn
Row 6: sl1, p9, p2tog, p1, turn
Row 7: knit across the 12 sts

With the free needle, pick up (see p. 8) 2 stitches down the side and knit across the 3 stitches from needle 2.

With the resulting free needle, knit 3 stitches from needle 3 and pick up 2 more stitches from the other side:

Needle 1: 12 sts
Needle 2: 5 sts
Needle 3: 5 sts

Rearrange the stitches as follows:

Needles 1 and 2: 7 sts
Needle 3: 8 sts

Change back to working in the round:

Next round: knit to last 2 sts, k2tog (7 sts per needle, 21 stitches total)

Place a stitch marker on the last round and leave it there.

Knit every round until the leg measures 1¾ inches from the stitch marker.

Next round: (k5, k2tog), repeat on each needle (6 sts per needle, 18 sts total remain)

Bind off, leaving tails free.

feet (make 2)

With Quebracho Bark, cast on 9 stitches, placing 3 stitches on each of three double-pointed needles. Join to work in the round, being careful not to twist the stitches. Place a stitch marker on the first stitch.

Rounds 1 and 2: knit
Round 3: kfb in each stitch (6 sts per needle, 18 sts total)

Knit every round until the foot measures 1 inch from the cast-on stitches.

Next round: (k2, kfb), repeat to end of round (8 sts per needle, 24 sts total)

Knit every round until the foot measures 2½ inches from the cast-on stitches.

Rearrange the stitches, placing 12 stitches on each of two double-pointed needles.

Next round: (ssk, k to last 2 sts, k2tog) on each needle (10 sts per needle, 20 sts total remain)

Thread the tail from the cast-on edge on a yarn needle, stitch through all of the cast-on stitches, and gather to close the hole. Stitch to secure. Weave the end to the inside and trim. Fill the feet with poly pellets or fiberfill.

Cut the yarn, leaving a 12-inch-long end. Thread on a yarn needle and use kitchener stitch to graft the foot.

With the remaining tail, take 4 stitches about ¼ inch in from the tip of the foot to create toes.

Whipstitch the feet to the bottom of the legs using a yarn needle and the bound-off tails from the legs. Stuff the legs with fiberfill. Whipstitch the top of the legs closed using the cast-on tail, then whipstitch the legs to the body, using the photograph as a guide. When attached to the body, the legs should bow out and the feet should bend inward.

nose and belly button (make 1 each)

With Quebracho Bark and two double-pointed needles used as straight needles, cast on 1 stitch loosely.

Row 1: kfb and then in the front again (3 sts)
Row 2: knit
Row 3: purl
Row 4: knit, do not turn, pass the second and third stitches over the first stitch and off the needle. Cut the yarn and pull through the remaining stitch. Thread the tail on a yarn needle, stitch around the edge of the piece, and gather the stitches to create a tiny ball. Whipstitch the nose to the center of the face and whipstitch the belly button to the stomach, about 2 inches up from the bottom of the seated body.

eyes and mouth

With an embroidery needle and brown embroidery floss, make two spiderweb circles (see p. 13) for the eyes. Add three eyelashes to the outer sides with straight stitches (see p. 14). With the white embroidery floss take a tiny straight stitch in each eye.

Take 2 straight stitches with brown embroidery floss for the eyebrows. Take 4 straight stitches in a curved line for the mouth.

ruffle pants

front

With Natural and the 24-inch circular needle or straight needles, cast on 38 stitches.
Rows 1 and 2: (k1, p1), repeat to end of row
Change to working in stockinette stitch (knit 1 row, purl 1 row), and continue until the front measures 2 inches from the cast-on edge, ending with a purl row.

Decrease rows

Bind off 2 stitches at the beginning of the next 4 rows (30 sts remain).

Bind off 3 stitches at the beginning of the next 8 rows (6 sts remain).

Cut the yarn, leaving the remaining stitches on the needle, and set aside.

back

Work the same as for the front, but work in stockinette stitch until the back measures 3 inches from the cast-on edge.

Decrease the same as for the front (6 sts remain).

Cut the yarn, leaving an 8-inch-long tail, and thread on a yarn needle.

Place the front and back pieces together, purl sides facing, and use mattress stitch (see p. 00) to sew the side seams.

On the back of the pants, measure down the side seam 2 inches from the waistband. Bring back corner up to meet front corner to create a dart on the back. Whipstitch the dart with a length of Natural threaded on a yarn needle. Tack down the fold on the inside with a couple of stitches to secure.

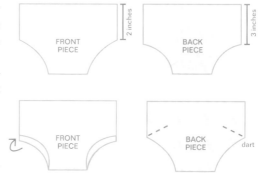

leg edging (2 options)

With the crochet hook and a length of Natural, single crochet in every other stitch around the leg opening. Cut the yarn and pull through the remaining stitch. Weave the ends to the inside.

With the smaller double-pointed needles, pick up stitches in every other stitch around the leg opening. As you are picking up stitches, work them evenly onto three double-pointed needles. Knit 1 round. Bind off. Cut the yarn and pull through the remaining stitch. Weave the ends to the inside and trim.

ruffle (make 2)

With Natural and a 24-inch circular needle or straight needles, cast on 21 stitches.

Row 1: kfb in each stitch (42 sts)

Row 2: purl

Row 3: knit

Row 4: purl

Row 5:: (k1, p1) repeat to end of row

Bind off. Cut the yarn, leaving an 8-inch-long tail. Thread the tail on a yarn needle and whip-stitch the first ruffle to the back of the pants under the ribbing. Attach the second ruffle under the first in the same way.

hat

With the 12-inch circular needle and Madder, cast on 64 stitches. Join to work in the round, being careful not to twist the stitches. Place a stitch marker on the first stitch.

Knit every round until the hat measures 2½ inches from the cast-on edge.

Decrease rounds

Knit the first round onto three double-pointed needles.

Round 1:

Needles 1 and 2: (k6, k2tog), repeat 3 times on each needle (21 sts per needle remain)

Needle 3: (k6, k2tog), repeat 2 times (14 sts remain)

56 stitches total remain.

Round 2: (k5, k2tog), repeat to end of round (18 sts on needles 1 and 2, 12 sts on needle 3; 48 sts total remain)

Rounds 3 and 4: knit

Round 5: (k4, k2tog), repeat to end of round (15 sts on needles 1 and 2, 10 sts on needle 3; 40 sts total remain)

Round 6: knit

Round 7: (k3, k2tog), repeat to end of round (12 sts on needles 1 and 2, 8 sts on needle 3; 32 sts total remain)

Round 8: knit

Round 9: (k2, k2tog), repeat to end of round (9 sts on needles 1 and 2, 6 sts on needle 3; 24 sts total remain)

Round 10: (k1, k2tog), repeat to end of round (6 sts on needles 1 and 2, 4 sts on needle 3; 16 sts total remain)

Round 11: k2tog, repeat to end of round (3 sts on needles 1 and 2, 2 sts on needle 3; 8 sts total remain)

Knit the next round onto one double-pointed needle.

Round 12: k2tog, repeat to end of round (4 sts remain)

Switch to Lipstick Tree and on the remaining 4 stitches begin to work in I-cord (see p. 7) as follows:

Row 1: k1, k2tog, k1 (3 sts remain)

Continue working in I-cord until the piece measures 1 inch from the beginning. Bind off. Cut the yarn and pull through the remaining stitch. Thread the tail on a yarn needle and tack down the end with a couple of stitches to form a loop. Weave the end to the inside of the hat and trim. Weave the rest of the ends to the inside and trim.

braids (make 2)

Cut 21 8-inch-long strands of Yellowwood. Place the hat on the Baby Doll's head and mark the placement of the braids with a pin or stitch marker. The braids should fall just in front of the ears.

Threading 3 strands at a time on a yarn needle, pull through a purl loop at the marker and where the hat naturally rolls up at the brim. Pull the strands halfway through.

Divide the hair into three 7-strand segments and braid. With a length of yarn, tie the ends of the braids with a knot and then a double-tied bow. Trim the ends of the braids to the desired length.

sundress

With Lipstick Tree and the 16-inch circular needle, cast on 120 stitches. Join to work in the round, being careful not to twist the stitches. Place a stitch marker on the first stitch.

Rounds 1–3: knit

Round 4: purl

Switch to Madder.
Rounds 5–8: knit

Switch to Lipstick Tree.
Rounds 9–12: knit

NOTE • Carry the colors along the inside as you work, and be sure not to pull too tightly as you knit.

Repeat rounds 9–12 three more times and then rounds 5–8 one more time.

Next round: k2tog, repeat to end of round, and at the same time work onto three double-pointed needles (20 sts per needle, 60 sts total remain)
Next 3 rounds: Work in 1 x 1 rib: (k1, p1), repeat to end of round

Bind off loosely in rib. Cut the yarn and pull through the remaining stitch.

straps (make 2)

With Lipstick Tree and two double-pointed needles used as straight needles, cast on 5 stitches. Work in garter stitch (knit every row) until the strap measures 4½ inches from the cast-on edge. Bind off. With a yarn needle and the strap tails, whipstitch the straps ½ inch down from the top edge of the dress and about 1½ inches in from the sides.

girl's hat

With Madder and the 16-inch circular needle, cast on 99 stitches. Join to work in the round, being careful not to twist the stitches. Place a stitch marker on the first stitch.

Knit every round until the hat measures 6½ inches from the cast-on edge.

Decrease rounds
Round 1: (k7, k2tog), repeat to end of round (88 sts remain)
Round 2: (k6, k2tog), repeat to end of round (77 sts remain)
Round 3: (k5, k2tog), repeat to end of round (66 sts remain)
Round 4: knit

For the next round, work onto three double-pointed needles as follows:
Round 5: (k4, k2tog), repeat to end of round (20 sts on needles 1 and 2, 15 sts on needle 3; 55 sts remain)
Round 6: knit
Round 7: (k3, k2tog), repeat to end of round (16 sts on needles 1 and 2, 12 sts on needle 3; 44 sts remain)
Round 8: (k2, k2tog), repeat to end of round (12 sts on needles 1 and 2, 9 sts on needle 3; 33 sts remain)
Round 9: knit
Round 10: (k1, k2tog), repeat to end of round (8 sts on needles 1 and 2, 6 sts on needle 3; 22 sts remain)
Round 11: knit
Round 12: k2tog, repeat to end of round (4 sts on needles 1 and 2, 3 sts on needle 3; 11 sts remain)
Round 13:
Needles 1 and 2: (k1, k2tog, k1), repeat on each needle (3 sts per needle remain)
Needle 3: knit (3 sts)
Round 14: (k1, k2tog), repeat on each needle (2 sts per needle remain)

Switch to Lipstick Tree and place all 6 remaining stitches on one double-pointed needle. Begin to work in I-cord.
Row 1: k2tog, k2, k2tog (4 sts remain)

Continue working in I-cord until the cord measures 3 inches from the beginning. Bind off. Cut the yarn and pull through the remaining stitch. Thread the bound-off tail on a yarn needle and whipstitch the end to the top center of the hat. Bring the other end of the cord around to meet the first, and tack down with a few more stitches to form a loop. Weave the tail to the inside of the hat and trim. Weave in all other remaining tails and trim.

braids

Complete the same as for the Baby Doll's hat, but use 30 6-inch strands. Divide into groups of 10 for braiding. Trim to desired length.

7

reversibles

When I went on tour for my second book, *Itty-Bitty Nursery*, I brought along a couple of my reversible toys to share with knitters I met on my travels. The enthusiastic reaction to these projects—the oohs and aahs and the laughter—was amazing, and the stir almost indescribable.

Reversibles are appealing to both adults and kids. You are going to love the simplicity of knitting reversibles and the pure joy the results will bring. All of the projects offered in this chapter are easy enough for beginners while still being interesting enough for advanced knitters. In case it isn't your cup of tea, every time there is some easy crochet involved, I offer a knitted option to use instead.

I've included a turtle and a frog, and an egg that becomes a little bluebird. I made all of the reversible projects in the most beautiful organic cotton and wool blend by O-Wool. One skein of each of the colors used throughout the chapter will give you enough yarn to make all five of the projects, because the colors overlap between them. Have fun and just wait for the joyous reaction your reversibles will bring!

frog and turtle

I had to include some water-loving friends in the reversibles collection. I have a thing for turtles and frogs in knitted form, as you may have seen in my other books.

The turtle has a subtle appliqué flower on top of her shell. (But if appliqué isn't your thing, the turtle is just as cute plain and simple.)

The frog features some fantastic curlicue legs, and his froggy toes really make him come to life. Such little details can really take a toy over the top and make it something special to keep forever.

finished measurements

- 6 inches tall, 5 inches wide

yarn

- O-Wool Balance (50% certified organic merino wool, 50% certified organic cotton; 130 yards/50 grams)
- Frog: 1 skein in Peridot #3017 and a small amount of Jade #3125 for the face embroidery
- Turtle: 1 skein each in Peridot #3017 and Jade #3125

tools

- U.S. size 4 set of four double-pointed needles, or size needed to obtain gauge
- Tape measure or ruler
- Yarn needle
- Stitch markers
- Scissors
- Polyester fiberfill, 1 small bag
- U.S. size F crochet hook (optional)
- Pins

gauge

- 6 stitches per inch in stockinette stitch

frog

body

With Peridot, cast on 60 stitches, leaving a long tail and placing 20 stitches on each of three double-pointed needles. Join to work in the round, being careful not to twist the stitches. Place a stitch marker on the first stitch.

Rounds 1 and 2: knit

Round 3: purl

Continue to knit every round until the body measures 3 inches from the purl round.

Decrease rounds

Round 1: (k8, k2tog), repeat to end of round (18 sts per needle, 54 sts total remain)

Round 2: (k7, k2tog), repeat to end of round (16 sts per needle, 48 sts total remain)

Rounds 3 and 4: knit

Round 5: (k6, k2tog), repeat to end of round (14 sts per needle, 42 sts total remain)

Round 6: (k5, k2tog), repeat to end of round (12 sts per needle, 36 sts total remain)

Round 7: knit

Round 8: (k4, k2tog), repeat to end of round (10 sts per needle, 30 sts total remain)

Round 9: (k3, k2tog), repeat to end of round (8 sts per needle, 24 sts total remain)

Round 10: (k2, k2tog), repeat to end of round (6 sts per needle, 18 sts total remain)

Round 11: (k1, k2tog), repeat to end of round (4 sts per needle, 12 sts total remain)

Round 12: k2tog, repeat to end of round (2 sts per needle, 6 sts total remain)

Cut the yarn and thread the tail on a yarn needle. Pull the end through the remaining stitches,

gather up tight to close the hole, and stitch to secure. Leave the tail free to use later for attaching the head.

Thread the tail from the cast-on stitches on a yarn needle. Turn the body inside out, and turn up the cast-on edge toward the wrong (purl) side of the body, using the purl round as a turning edge. With a length of Peridot threaded on a yarn needle, whipstitch the cast-on edge to the inside of the body. Weave in the end and trim.

head

Starting at the bottom of the head with Peridot, cast on 9 stitches, placing 3 stitches on each of three double-pointed needles. Join to work in the round, being careful not to twist the stitches. Place a stitch marker on the first stitch.

Round 1: knit

Round 2: kfb in each stitch (6 sts per needle, 18 sts total)

Round 3: knit

Round 4: kfb in each stitch (12 sts per needle, 36 sts total)

Rounds 5–7: knit

Round 8: (k2, kfb), repeat to end of round (16 sts per needle, 48 sts total)

Rounds 9–18: knit

Decrease rounds (for the top of the head)

Round 19: (k2, k2tog), repeat to end of round (12 sts per needle, 36 sts total remain)

Rounds 20 and 21: knit

Round 22: (k1, k2tog), repeat to end of round (8 sts per needle, 24 sts total remain)

Rounds 23 and 24: knit

Thread the tail from the cast-on stitches on a yarn needle. Stitch through all of the cast-on stitches, gather tightly to close the hole on the back of the head, and stitch to secure. Weave the end to the inside and trim.

Stuff the head with fiberfill.

Round 25: k2tog, repeat to end of round (4 sts per needle, 12 sts total remain)

Round 26: (k1, k2tog, k1), repeat on each needle (3 sts per needle, 9 sts remain)

Finish stuffing. Cut the yarn and thread the end on a yarn needle. Pull through the remaining stitches, gather up tight to close the hole, and stitch to secure. Weave the end to the inside and trim.

With the tail from the body threaded on a yarn needle, whipstitch the head to the body at the cast-on end. Weave the end to the inside and trim.

eyes (make 2)

With Peridot, cast on 15 stitches, placing 5 stitches on each of three double-pointed needles. Join to work in the round, being careful not to twist the stitches. Place a stitch marker on first stitch.

Rounds 1–3: knit

Round 4: (k3, k2tog), repeat on each needle (4 sts per needle, 12 sts total remain)

Round 5: knit

Round 6: (k2, k2tog), repeat on each needle (3 sts per needle, 9 sts total remain)

Cut the yarn and thread the end on a yarn needle. Pull through the remaining stitches, gather up tight to close the hole, and stitch to secure. Weave the end to the inside and trim.

Stuff the eyes with fiberfill. Thread the tail from the cast-on edge on a yarn needle and whipstitch the eyes to the top of the head, using the photograph as a guide.

arms (make 2)

With Peridot and two double-pointed needles used as straight needles, cast on 3 stitches. Work in I-cord (see p. 00) until the arm measures 3½ inches from the cast-on edge.

Continue on to create the toes:

Next round: kfb in the first stitch; with a free double-pointed needle, work in I-cord (see p. 7) on these 2 stitches only for ½ inch. Bind off. Cut the yarn and pull through the remaining stitch.

Reattach the yarn and complete the same way for each of the remaining 2 stitches. You will have 3 toes.

Weave in all ends. Thread the tail from the cast-on stitches on a yarn needle. Whipstitch the arms to the body at the neck and tack down the arm from shoulder to wrist, using the photograph as a guide.

legs (make 2)

Work as for the arms and toes, but work the I-cord for 5 inches before starting the toes.

Arrange the legs in a swirl and whipstitch to the back side of the body, using the photograph as a guide.

eyes and mouth

With a length of Jade threaded on a yarn needle, make 2 straight stitches (see p. 14) for each eye and make 4 wraps (see p. 15) around the straight stitches. Create the mouth with straight stitches, and then wrap each stitch several times.

turtle

body (shell)

With Jade, complete the body the same as for the frog.

head

Starting at the bottom of the head with Peridot, cast on 9 stitches, placing 3 stitches on each of three double-pointed needles. Join to work in the round, being careful not to twist the stitches. Place a stitch marker on the first stitch.

Round 1: knit

Round 2: kfb in each stitch (6 sts per needle, 18 sts total)

Round 3: knit

Round 4: kfb in each stitch (12 sts per needle, 36 sts total)

Rounds 5–12: knit

Decrease rounds

Round 13: (k2, k2tog), repeat to end of round (9 sts per needle, 27 sts total remain)

Rounds 14 and 15: knit

Round 16: (k1, k2tog), repeat to end of round (6 sts per needle, 18 sts total remain)

Thread the end from the cast-on stitches on a yarn needle. Stitch through all of the cast-on stitches, gather up tight to close the hole on the back of head, and stitch to secure. Weave the tail to the inside and trim.

Stuff the head with fiberfill.

Round 17: knit

Round 18: (k2tog), repeat to end of round (3 sts per needle, 9 sts total remain)

Finish stuffing. Cut the yarn and thread the tail on a yarn needle. Pull through the remaining stitches, gather up tight to close the hole, and stitch to secure. Weave the tail to the inside and trim.

With the tail from the body threaded on a yarn needle, whipstitch the head to the body so the back of the head meets the shell. (The cast-on stitches will be on the bottom of the head and the decrease rounds will be on top.) Weave the tail to the inside and trim.

feet (make 4)

With Peridot, cast on 12 stitches, placing 4 stitches on each of three double-pointed needles. Join to work in the round, being careful not to twist the stitches. Place a stitch marker on the first stitch.

Knit every round until the foot measures 1 inch from the cast-on edge.

Next round: (k2, k2tog), repeat on each needle (3 sts per needle, 9 sts total remain)

Next round: (k1, k2tog), repeat on each needle (2 sts per needle, 6 sts total remain)

Cut the yarn and thread on a yarn needle. Pull through the remaining stitches, pull up tight to close the hole, and stitch to secure. Weave the end to the inside and trim. Stuff feet lightly and whipstitch the cast-on edges closed. Leave the tail free.

With the cast-on tail threaded on a yarn needle, whipstitch the feet to the lower edges of the body, using the photograph as a guide.

tail

With Peridot and two double-pointed needles used as straight needles, cast on 3 stitches. Work in I-cord until the tail measures 1 inch from the cast-on stitches.

Next row: k2tog (1 st remains)

Cut the yarn and pull the end through the remaining stitch. Thread the tail from the cast-on stitches on a yarn needle. Whipstitch the tail to the center lower back of the shell, between the back feet. Weave the ends to the inside.

flower for the top of the shell

center

With Peridot, cast 6 stitches, placing 2 stitches on each of three double-pointed needles. Join to work in the round, being careful not to twist the stitches. Place a stitch marker on the first stitch.

Round 1: knit

Round 2: kfb in each stitch (4 sts per needle, 12 sts total)

Round 3: knit

Bind off. Cut the yarn and pull the end through the last stitch. Thread the tail from the cast-on stitches on a yarn needle, stitch through all the

cast-on stitches, and gather to close up the hole. Stitch to secure. Weave the tail to the inside and trim. Place the tail from the bound-off stitches on a yarn needle and whipstitch the center to the top middle of the shell.

petals (make 7)

With Peridot and two double-pointed needles used as straight needles, cast on 3 stitches.

Row 1: knit
Row 2: purl
Row 3: k1, m1, k1, m1, k1 (5 sts)
Row 4: purl
Row 5: knit
Row 6: purl
Row 7: ssk, k1, k2tog (3 sts remain)

Bind off. Cut the yarn and pull the end through the remaining stitch.

Arrange and pin the petals around the center, leaving some space between them. With a yarn needle and the tails, whipstitch the petals to the shell. Weave in ends to the wrong side and trim.

rectangles (make 6)

With Peridot and two double-pointed needles used as straight needles, cast on 6 stitches. Work 4 rows in stockinette stitch (knit one row, purl one row). Bind off. Cut the yarn and pull the end through the remaining stitch.

With the tails threaded on a yarn needle, whipstitch the rectangles around the sides of the shell, using the photograph as a guide. Weave all ends to the inside and trim.

eyes and mouth

With a length of Jade threaded on a yarn needle, take one small straight stitch (see p. 14) for each eye and wrap each stitch 3 times (see p. 15). To create the mouth, take several straight stitches and wrap each stitch 3 times. Weave the ends to the inside and trim.

finishing

Turn the frog and the turtle inside out. With the heads lined up and facing in opposite directions, and the wrong sides touching, take a few stitches with matching yarn and the yarn needle at the tops of the bodies. This will prevent the two animals from pulling apart. Turn the toy so the frog is on the outside.

With Peridot and the crochet hook, slip stitch (see p. 12) through the purl (turning) rounds of both animals to join them at the bottom edge.

noncrochet alternative

With a length of Peridot threaded on a yarn needle, whipstitch through both animals' purl (turning) rounds to hold the two together. Weave all ends to the inside and trim.

lion and elephant

I have designed several knitted elephants, and it's always fun to make them—maybe on account of the distinctive trunk. This one is especially sweet, and you can play with the details by creating either crocheted or knitted ears.

The lion is the first I have designed, and the I-cord mane is absolutely worth the effort to make. Add his completely infectious smile, and you have a toy that will be the "pride" of any little one's collection.

This wild pair has teamed up to make perfect reversible buddies.

finished measurements

- 6 inches tall, 5 inches wide

yarn

- O-Wool Balance (50% certified organic merino wool, 50% certified organic cotton; 130 yards/50 grams)
- Lion: 1 skein each in Amber #6122 and Agate #8014, and a small amount of Opal #2026 (for the face embroidery)
- Elephant: 1 skein each in Opal #2026 and Slate #2215

tools

- U.S. size 4 set of four double-pointed needles, or size needed to obtain gauge
- U.S. size F crochet hook (optional)
- Tape measure or ruler
- Yarn needle
- Stitch markers
- Scissors
- Polyester fiberfill, 1 small bag

gauge

- 6 stitches per inch in stockinette stitch

lion

body

With Amber, cast on 60 stitches, leaving a long tail and placing 20 stitches on each of three double-pointed needles. Join to work in the round, being careful not to twist the stitches. Place a stitch marker on the first stitch.

Rounds 1 and 2: knit

Round 3: purl

Continue to knit every round until the body measures 3 inches from the purl round.

Decrease rounds

Round 1: (k8, k2tog), repeat to end of round (18 sts per needle, 54 sts total remain)

Round 2: (k7, k2tog), repeat to end of round (16 sts per needle, 48 sts total remain)

Rounds 3 and 4: knit

Round 5: (k6, k2tog), repeat to end of round (14 sts per needle, 42 sts total remain)

Round 6: (k5, k2tog), repeat to end of round (12 sts per needle, 36 sts total remain)

Round 7: knit

Round 8: (k4, k2tog), repeat to end of round (10 sts per needle, 30 sts total remain)

Round 9: (k3, k2tog), repeat to end of round (8 sts per needle, 24 sts total remain)

Round 10: (k2, k2tog), repeat to end of round (6 sts per needle, 18 sts total remain)

Round 11: (k1, k2tog), repeat to end of round (4 sts per needle, 12 sts total remain)

Round 12: k2tog, repeat to end of round (2 sts per needle, 6 sts total remain)

Cut the yarn and thread the tail on a yarn needle. Pull the end through the remaining stitches, gather up tight to close the hole, and stitch to secure. Leave the tail free to use later in attaching the head.

Thread the tail from the cast-on stitches on a yarn needle. Turn the body inside out, and turn up the cast-on edge toward the wrong (purl) side of the body, using the purl round as a turning edge. With a length of Amber threaded on a yarn needle, whipstitch the cast-on edge to the inside of the body. Weave in the end and trim.

head

Starting at the back of the head with Amber, cast on 9 stitches, placing 3 stitches on each of three double-pointed needles. Join to work in the round, being careful not to twist the stitches. Place a stitch marker on the first stitch.

Round 1: knit

Round 2: kfb in each stitch (6 sts per needle, 18 sts total)

Round 3: knit

Round 4: kfb in each stitch (12 sts per needle, 36 sts total)

Rounds 5–7: knit

Round 8: (k2, kfb), repeat to end of round (16 sts per needle, 48 sts total)

Rounds 9–18: knit

Decrease rounds (for the face)

Round 19: (k2, k2tog), repeat to end of round (12 sts per needle, 36 sts total remain)

Rounds 20 and 21: knit

Round 22: (k1, k2tog), repeat to end of round (8 sts per needle, 24 sts total remain)

Rounds 23 and 24: knit

Thread the tail from the cast-on stitches on a yarn needle. Stitch through all of the cast-on stitches, gather tightly to close the hole on the back of the head, and stitch to secure. Weave the end to the inside and trim.

Stuff the head with fiberfill.

Round 25: k2tog, repeat to end of round (4 sts per needle, 12 sts total remain)

Round 26: (k1, k2tog, k1), repeat on each needle (3 sts per needle, 9 sts remain)

Finish stuffing. Cut the yarn and thread the tail on a yarn needle. Pull through the remaining stitches, pull up tight to close the hole, and stitch to secure. Weave the tail to the inside and trim.

With the tail from the body threaded on a yarn needle, whipstitch the head to the body. Weave the tail to the inside and trim.

arms, feet, and ears (make 6 total)

With Amber, cast on 12 stitches, placing 4 stitches on each of three double-pointed needles. Join to work in the round, being careful not to twist the stitches. Place a stitch marker on the first stitch.

Knit every round until the arm or foot measures 1 inch from the cast-on edge.

Next round: (k2, k2tog), repeat on each needle (3 sts per needle, 9 sts total remain)

Next round: (k1, k2tog), repeat on each needle (2 sts per needle, 6 sts total remain)

finishing arms and feet

Cut the yarn, and place the end on a yarn needle. Pull through the remaining stitches and pull up tight to close the hole. Pull the end to the inside and trim to stay inside. Stuff lightly and whipstitch the cast-on edge closed.

With the tail threaded on a yarn needle, whipstitch the arms to the sides of the body and the feet to the bottom front of the body.

finishing ears

Finish as for the arms and feet, but do not stuff the ears. Pinch the cast-on edge together to create a fold, and secure with a couple of stitches. Whipstitch the folded ears to the head using the photograph as a guide.

tail

With Amber and two double-pointed needles used as straight needles, cast on 3 stitches. Work in I-cord (see p. 7) until the tail measures 2 inches from the cast-on edge.

Switch to Agate.

Continue working in I-cord until the tail measures 3 inches from the cast-on edge. Bind off. Cut the yarn and pull the end through the remaining stitch. Place the end on a yarn needle, weave through to the inside of the cord, and trim. Tie a knot in the Agate end of the cord.

Thread the tail from the cast-on stitches on a yarn needle and whipstitch the tail to the lower center back. Weave the end to the inside and trim.

mane (make 17 strands)

With Agate and two double-pointed needles used as straight needles, cast on 3 stitches. Work in I-cord until the strand of mane measures 2½ inches from the cast-on edge. Bind off. Tie a knot in the end, weave in the tail, and trim.

Using the photograph as a guide, whipstitch the I-cords around the face area and behind the ears with the cast-on tails threaded on a yarn needle. Weave the ends to the inside and trim.

face

With a length of Opal and the yarn needle, take 2 straight stitches (see p. 14) for each eye. With the photograph as a guide, use satin stitch (see p. 14) for the nose and backstitch (see p. 13) for one side of the mouth.

elephant
body

With Opal, complete the body the same as for the lion.

head

Starting at the back of the head with Opal, complete the head the same as for the lion through round 25.

Continue on to create the trunk:
Rounds 26–30: knit
Round 31: (k1, k2tog, k1), repeat on each needle (3 sts per needle, 9 sts total remain)
Rounds 32–43: knit
   Stuff the trunk.
Round 44: purl
Round 45: knit

Finish stuffing.

   Cut the yarn and thread the tail on a yarn needle. Pull through the remaining stitches, gather up tight to close the hole, and stitch to secure.

With the tail from the body threaded on a yarn needle, whipstitch the head to the top of the body. Tack the trunk down to the front of the body with a couple of stitches. Weave all of the ends to the inside and trim.

ears (make 2)
crocheted option

With Opal and the crochet hook, chain 4 (see p. 11) and join with a slip stitch (see p. 12) to make a loop.

Round 1: single crochet (see p. 12) 8 sts in the center of the loop
Round 2: chain 1, (single crochet 1 in the next stitch, single crochet 2 sts in the next st) repeat ( ) to the end of the round. Join with a slip stitch.
Round 3: chain 1, (single crochet 1 in the next 2 sts, single crochet 2 sts in the next st), repeat ( ) to the end of the round. Join with a slip stitch.
Round 4: chain 1, (single crochet 1 in the next 3 sts, single crochet 2 sts in the next st) repeat ( ) to the end of the round. Join with a slip stitch.
Round 5: chain 1, (single crochet 1 in the next 4 sts, single crochet 2 sts in the next st) repeat ( ) to the end of the round. Join with a slip stitch.

   Cut the yarn and pull the end through the remaining stitch. Fold the ear in half. With Slate, single crochet along the edges of the ear to seam the two layers together. Cut the yarn and pull through the remaining stitch. Weave the end to the inside and trim.

With a length of Opal threaded on a yarn needle, whipstitch the folded edge of the ears to the sides of the head. Weave in the ends.

knitted option

With Opal, cast on 18 stitches, leaving a long tail and placing 6 stitches on each of three double-pointed needles. Join to work in the round, being careful not to twist the stitches. Place a stitch marker on the first stitch.

   Knit every round until the ear measures 1 inch from the cast-on edge.

Decrease rounds
Round 1: (k4, k2tog), repeat on each needle (5 sts per needle, 15 sts total remain)
Round 2: (k3, k2tog), repeat on each needle (4 sts per needle, 12 sts total remain)
Round 3: knit
Round 4: (k2, k2tog), repeat on each needle (3 sts per needle, 9 sts total remain)

   Cut the yarn and thread the tail on a yarn needle. Pull the end through the remaining stitches, gather up tight to close the hole, and stitch to secure. Thread the tail from the cast-on stitches on a yarn needle and whipstitch the cast-on edge

closed. Whipstitch the ears to the sides of the head. Weave all ends to the inside and trim.

arms and legs (make 4 total)
With Opal, complete the arms and legs the same as for the lion.

tail
With Slate, cut three 12-inch strands and thread all three on a yarn needle. Pull the strands through the lower center back, drawing them through only halfway. Braid the strands, using three groups of two strands held together. Tie a knot in the end and trim the ends.

eyes
With a length of Slate threaded on a yarn needle, Take 2 straight stitches and then wrap the stitches 5 times for each eye.

finishing
Turn the lion and the elephant inside out. With the heads lined up and facing in opposite directions, and the wrong sides touching, take a few stitches with matching yarn and the yarn needle at the tops of the bodies. This will prevent the two animals from pulling apart. Turn the toy so the elephant is on the outside.

With Opal and the crochet hook, slip stitch through the purl (turning) rounds of both animals to join them at the bottom edge.

noncrochet alternative
With a length of Opal threaded on a yarn needle, whipstitch through the purl (turning) rounds of both animals to join them at the bottom edge. Weave all ends to the inside and trim.

cat and mouse

The cat and mouse reversible is the first toy I made for this collection. I was so thrilled with the result that I couldn't wait to start the next one. It's a beginner-friendly toy with simple and repetitive shapes and minimal seaming, which are always a plus. You will knit these two up in no time at all.

- 6 inches tall, 5 inches wide

- O-Wool Balance (50% certified organic merino wool, 50% certified organic cotton; 130 yards/50 grams)
- Mouse: 1 skein each in Natural #1000 and Rose Quartz #4105, and a small amount of Slate #2215 for the face embroidery
- Cat: 1 skein each in Slate #2215 and Amber #6122

- U.S. size 4 set of four double-pointed needles, or size needed to obtain gauge
- U.S. size F crochet hook (optional)
- Tape measure or ruler
- Yarn needle
- Stitch markers
- Scissors
- Polyester fiberfill, 1 small bag

- 6 stitches per inch in stockinette stitch

mouse

body

With Natural, cast on 60 stitches, leaving a long tail and placing 20 stitches on each of three double-pointed needles. Join to work in the round, being careful not to twist the stitches. Place a stitch marker on the first stitch.

Rounds 1 and 2: knit

Round 3: purl

Continue to knit every round until the body measures 3 inches from the purl round.

Decrease rounds

Round 1: (k8, k2tog), repeat to end of round (18 sts per needle, 54 sts total remain)

Round 2: (k7, k2tog), repeat to end of round (16 sts per needle, 48 sts total remain)

Round 3 and 4: knit

Round 5: (k6, k2tog), repeat to end of round (14 sts per needle, 42 sts total remain)

Round 6: (k5, k2tog), repeat to end of round (12 sts per needle, 36 sts total remain)

Round 7: knit

Round 8: (k4, k2tog), repeat to end of round (10 sts per needle, 30 sts total remain)

Round 9: (k3, k2tog), repeat to end of round (8 sts per needle, 24 sts total remain)

Round 10: (k2, k2tog), repeat to end of round (6 sts per needle, 18 sts total remain)

Round 11: (k1, k2tog), repeat to end of round (4 sts per needle, 12 sts total remain)

Round 12: k2tog, repeat to end of round (2 sts per needle, 6 sts total remain)

Cut the yarn and thread the tail on a yarn needle. Pull the end through the remaining stitches, gather up tight to close the hole, and stitch to secure. Leave the tail free to use later in attaching the head.

Thread the tail from the cast-on stitches on a yarn needle. Turn the body inside out, and turn up the cast-on edge toward the wrong (purl) side of the body, using the purl round as a turning edge. With a length of Natural threaded on a yarn needle, whipstitch the cast-on edge to the inside of the body. Weave in the end and trim.

head

Starting at the back of the head with Natural, cast on 9 stitches, placing 3 stitches on each of three double-pointed needles. Join to work in the round, being careful not to twist the stitches. Place a stitch marker on the first stitch.
Round 1: knit
Round 2: kfb in each stitch (6 sts per needle, 18 sts total)
Round 3: knit
Round 4: kfb in each stitch (12 sts per needle, 36 sts total)
Rounds 5–7: knit
Round 8: (k2, kfb), repeat to end of round (16 sts per needle, 48 sts total)
Rounds 9–18: knit

Decrease rounds (for the nose)
Round 19: (k2, k2tog), repeat to end of round (12 sts per needle, 36 sts total remain)
Rounds 20 and 21: knit
Round 22: (k1, k2tog), repeat to end of round (8 sts per needle, 24 sts total remain)
Rounds 23–25: knit

Thread the tail from the cast-on stitches on a yarn needle. Stitch through all of the cast-on stitches, gather up tight to close the hole on the back of the head, and stitch to secure. Weave the end to the inside and trim.

Stuff the head with fiberfill.

Round 26: (k2, k2tog), repeat to end of round (6 sts per needle, 18 sts total remain)
Rounds 27–29: knit
Round 30: (k1, k2tog), repeat to end of round (4 sts per needle, 12 sts total remain)
Rounds 31 and 32: knit
Finish stuffing.

Round 33: (k2tog), repeat to end of round (2 sts per needle, 6 sts total remain)

Cut the yarn and thread the tail on a yarn needle. Pull through the remaining stitches, gather up tight to close the hole, and stitch to secure. Weave the end to the inside of the head and trim.

With the long tail from the body cast-on edge threaded on a yarn needle, whipstitch the head to the body. Weave the end to the inside and trim.

nose tip

With Rose Quartz and two double-pointed needles used as straight needles, cast on 1 stitch loosely.
Row 1: kfb until there are 3 stitches on the right needle (3 sts)
Row 2: knit
Row 3: purl
Row 4: knit, do not turn, pass the second and third stitches over the first stitch and off the needle.

Cut the yarn and thread the end on a yarn needle. Take a few stitches around the edge of the piece, and gather up to make a ball. Attach the bobble to the tip of the nose with a few stitches. Weave the end to the inside and trim.

ears
outer ear (make 2)
With Natural and two double-pointed needles used as straight needles, cast on 12 stitches.

Work in stockinette stitch (knit 1 row, purl 1 row) until the ear measures 1½ inches from the cast-on edge.

Decrease rows (for the top of the ear)
Row 1: k1, ssk, k6, k2tog, k1 (10 sts remain)
Row 2: p1, p2tog, p4, p2tog, p1 (8 sts remain)
Row 3: k1, ssk, k2, k2tog, k1 (6 sts remain)
Row 4: p1, p2tog, p2tog, p1 (4 sts remain)
Bind off. Cut the yarn and pull through the remaining stitch. Set aside.

inner ear (make 2)
With Rose Quartz and two double-pointed needles used as straight needles, cast on 10 stitches.

Work in stockinette stitch until the ear measures 1¼ inches from the cast-on edge.

Decrease rows (for the top of the ear)

Row 1: k1, ssk, k4, k2tog, k1 (8 sts remain)
Row 2: p1, p2tog, p2, p2tog, p1 (6 sts remain)
Row 3: k1, ssk, k2tog, k1 (4 sts remain)
Row 4: p1, p2tog, p1 (3 sts remain)

Bind off. Cut the yarn and pull through the remaining stitch.

finishing

Place one inner ear piece on each outer ear piece, edges aligned with purl sides facing. With the inner ear tails threaded on a yarn needle, whipstitch around the edges of the ears. Fold the bottom edge of the ears in half widthwise to create a cupped shape. With a length of Natural threaded on a yarn needle, whipstitch the folded base of the ears to the head, using the photograph as a guide.

eyes

With a length of Slate threaded on a yarn needle, take 2 small straight stitches (see p. 14) for each eye.

arms and feet (make 4 total)

With Rose Quartz, cast on 9 stitches, placing 3 stitches on each of three double-pointed needles. Join to work in the round, being careful not to twist the stitches. Place a stitch marker on the first stitch.

Rounds 1–4: knit
Round 5: (k1, k2tog), repeat on each needle (2 sts per needle, 6 sts total remain)

Cut the yarn and thread on a yarn needle. Pull through the remaining stitches, gather up tight to close the hole, and stitch to secure. Weave the end to the inside and trim. Stuff lightly with fiberfill and whipstitch the cast-on edge closed with the tail.

With the tail threaded on a yarn needle, whipstitch the arms to the sides of the body and the feet to the bottom front of the body.

tail

With Natural and two double-pointed needles used as straight needles, cast on 3 stitches. Work in I-cord (see p. 7) until the tail measures 2½ inches from the cast-on edge.

Next row: k1, k2tog, do not turn, pass the first stitch over the second stitch and off the needle.

Cut the yarn and pull through the remaining stitch. Thread the tail from the cast-on edge on a yarn needle and whipstitch the tail to the lower center back. Weave the ends to the inside and trim.

cat
body
Begin with Slate and complete rounds 1–3 as for the mouse. Continue to make the body the same as for the mouse, and at the same time begin the stripe pattern. Carry the colors along the inside.

stripe pattern
Rounds 1–3: Slate
Rounds 4 and 5: Amber
Repeat rounds 1–5 to the decrease rounds. Complete the decrease rounds in Slate only.

head
Starting at the back of the head with Slate, cast on 9 stitches, placing 3 stitches on each of three double-pointed needles. Join to work in the round, being careful not to twist the stitches.

Place a stitch marker on the first stitch. Work in stripe pattern for rounds 1–18 as follows:
Rounds 1 and 2: Slate
Rounds 3 and 4: Amber

At the same time, repeat rounds 1–4 of the stripe pattern for the following rounds:
Round 1: knit

Round 2: kfb in each stitch (6 sts per needle, 18 sts total)
Round 3: knit
Round 4: kfb in each stitch (12 sts per needle, 36 sts total)
Rounds 5–7: knit
Round 8: (k2, kfb), repeat to end of round (16 sts per needle, 48 sts total)
Rounds 9–18: knit

Decrease rounds
Complete in Amber only.
Round 19: (k2, k2tog), repeat to end of round (12 sts per needle, 36 sts total remain)
Rounds 20 and 21: knit
Round 22: (k1, k2tog), repeat to end of round (8 sts per needle, 24 sts total remain)
Rounds 23 and 24: knit

Thread the tail from the cast-on edge on a yarn needle. Stitch through all of the cast-on stitches, gather tightly to close the hole on the back of head, and stitch to secure. Weave the end to the inside and trim.

Stuff the head with fiberfill.

Round 25: k2tog, repeat to end of round (4 sts per needle, 12 sts total remain)
Round 26: (k1, k2tog, k1), repeat on each needle (3 sts per needle, 9 sts remain)

Finish stuffing. Cut the yarn and thread the tail on a yarn needle. Pull through the remaining stitches, gather tightly to close the hole, and stitch to secure. Weave the end to the inside of the head and trim.

With the long tail from the body threaded on a yarn needle, whipstitch the head to the body. Weave the end to the inside and trim.

arms and feet (make 4 total)

With Slate, cast on 12 stitches, placing 4 stitches on each of three double-pointed needles. Join to work in the round, being careful not to twist the stitches. Place a stitch marker on the first stitch.

Knit every round until the piece measures 1 inch above the cast-on edge.

Next round: (k2, k2tog), repeat on each needle (3 sts per needle, 9 sts total remain)

Next round: (k1, k2tog), repeat on each needle (2 sts per needle, 6 sts total remain)

Cut the yarn and thread on a yarn needle. Pull through the remaining stitches, gather up tight to close the hole, and stitch to secure. Weave the end to the inside and trim. Stuff lightly and whipstitch the cast-on edge closed.

With the tails threaded on a yarn needle, whipstitch the arms to the sides of the body and the feet to the bottom front of the body.

ears (make 2)

With Slate, cast on 12 stitches, placing 4 stitches on each of three double-pointed needles. Join to work in the round, being careful not to twist the stitches. Place a stitch marker on the first stitch.

Rounds 1–3: knit

Round 4: (k2, k2tog), repeat on each needle (3 sts per needle, 9 sts total remain)

Round 5: knit

Round 6: (k1, k2tog), repeat on each needle (2 sts per needle, 6 sts total remain)

Round 7: knit

Round 8: k2tog, repeat on each needle (1 st per needle, 3 sts total remain)

Place the remaining 3 stitches on one double-pointed needle. Pass the second and third stitches over the first stitch and off the needle. Cut the yarn and thread the end on a yarn needle. Pull the end through the remaining stitch, weave to the inside, and trim. Thread the tail from the cast-on row on a yarn needle and whipstitch the cast-on edge closed. Whipstitch the ears to the head.

face

With a length of Slate threaded on a yarn needle, take one straight stitch with 4 wraps (see p. 15) for each eye, using the photograph as a guide. Use satin stitch (see p. 14) to create the nose. Use straight stitches with wraps to create the mouth.

tail

With Slate, cast on 9 stitches, placing 3 stitches on each of three double-pointed needles. Join to work in the round, being careful not to twist the stitches. Place a stitch marker on the first stitch.

Knit every round until the tail measures 2½ inches from the cast-on edge, and at the same time, work the stripe pattern.

stripe pattern

Rounds 1 and 2: Slate

Rounds 3 and 4: Amber

Repeat rounds 1–4 to the end of the tail.

Last round: (k1, k2tog), repeat to end of round (2 sts per needle, 6 sts total remain)

Cut the yarn and thread the tail on a yarn needle. Pull through the remaining stitches, gather up tight to close the hole, and stitch to secure. Weave the end to the inside and trim. Stuff the tail lightly with fiberfill. Thread the end from the cast-on stitches on a yarn needle. Whipstitch the tail to the center lower back. Weave all ends to the inside and trim.

finishing

Turn the cat and the mouse inside out, with the heads lined up and facing in opposite directions, and the wrong sides touching. Take a few stitches with matching yarn and yarn needle at the tops of the bodies, to prevent the two animals from pulling apart. Turn the toy so the mouse is on the outside.

With Natural and the crochet hook, slip stitch (see p. 12) through the purl (turning) rounds of both animals to join them at the bottom edge.

noncrochet alternative

With a length of Natural threaded on a yarn needle, whipstitch through the purl (turning) rounds of both animals to join them at the bottom edge. Weave all ends to the inside and trim.

sisters

I'll let you in on a secret: this set of dolls is an homage to my sister and me. We are joined together forever, just like this reversible toy.

My sister, Dawn, is the blonde and I'm the brunette. When we were little, my mom would always dress my sister in pink and red and I would always get the darker greens and blues. I always wanted to be the girl in the pink, but in this knitted version I kept the colors true to our childhood color schemes. The details make these little girls completely adorable.

This one is dedicated to my dear, sweet Dawn, my best friend forever in life.

finished measurements

- 6 inches tall, 3½ inches wide

yarn

- O-Wool Balance (50% certified organic merino wool, 50% certified organic cotton; 130 yards/50 grams), 1 skein each in Rose Quartz #4105, Slate #2215, Natural #1000, Agate #8014, and Amber #6122

tools

- U.S. size 4 set of four double-pointed needles, or size needed to obtain gauge
- U.S. size F crochet hook (optional)
- Tape measure or ruler
- Yarn needle
- Stitch markers
- Scissors
- Polyester fiberfill, 1 small bag
- Black and red embroidery floss

gauge

- 6 stitches per inch in stockinette stitch

dresses (make 2—one in Slate, one in Rose Quartz)

With Rose Quartz or Slate, cast on 45 stitches, leaving a long tail and placing 15 stitches on each of three double-pointed needles. Join to work in the round, being careful not to twist the stitches. Place a stitch marker on the first stitch.

Rounds 1 and 2: knit

Round 3: purl

Continue to knit every round until the body measures 2 inches from the purl round.

Decrease rounds

Round 1: (k1, ssk, k9, k2tog, k1), repeat on each needle (13 sts per needle, 39 sts total remain)

Rounds 2–9: knit

Round 10: (k1, ssk, k2, slip 1 stitch, k2tog, pass slipped stitch over, k2, k2tog, k1), repeat on each needle (9 sts per needle, 27 sts total remain)

Rounds 11–14: knit

Round 15: *k1, (k2, k2tog) twice, repeat from the * on each needle (7 sts per needle, 21 sts total remain)

Round 16: knit

Round 17: *k1, (k1, k2tog) twice, repeat from the * on each needle (5 sts per needle, 15 sts total remain)

Round 18: knit

Round 19: *k1, (k2tog) twice, repeat from the * on each needle (3 sts per needle, 9 sts total remain)

Round 20: knit

Cut the yarn and thread the tail on a yarn needle. Pull the end through the remaining stitches, gather up tight to close the hole, and stitch to secure. Weave the end to the inside and trim.

heads (make 2)

Starting at the bottom of the head with Natural, cast on 9 stitches, placing 3 stitches on each of three double-pointed needles. Join to work in the round, being careful not to twist the stitches. Place a stitch marker on the first stitch.

Round 1: knit

Round 2: (k1, m1, k1, m1, k1), repeat on each needle (5 sts per needle, 15 sts total)

Round 3: knit

Round 4: (k1, m1, k3, m1, k1), repeat on each needle (7 sts per needle, 21 sts total)

Round 5: knit

Round 6: (k1, m1, k5, m1, k1), repeat on each needle (9 sts per needle, 27 sts total)

Rounds 7–12: knit

Decrease rounds

Round 13: (k1, ssk, k3, k2tog, k1), repeat on each needle (7 sts per needle, 21 sts total remain)

Round 14: knit

Round 15: (k1, ssk, k1, k2tog, k1), repeat on each needle (5 sts per needle, 15 sts total remain)

Round 16: knit

Thread the tail from the cast-on edge on a yarn needle. Stitch through all of the cast-on stitches, gather up tight to close the hole on the back of head, and stitch to secure. Weave the end to the inside and trim.

Stuff the head with fiberfill.

Round 17: *k1 (k2tog) twice, repeat from the * on each needle (3 sts per needle, 9 sts total remain)

Round 18: knit

Finish stuffing. Cut the yarn, leaving an 8-inch-long tail, and thread on a yarn needle. Pull the end through the remaining stitches. Whipstitch the head to the top of the dress. Weave the end to the inside and trim.

rose quartz hat

With Rose Quartz, cast on 27 stitches, leaving a long tail and placing 9 stitches on each of three double-pointed needles. Join to work in the round, being careful not to twist the stitches. Place a stitch marker on the first stitch.

Knit every round until the hat measures 1½ inches from the cast-on edge.

Decrease rounds

Round 1: *k1, (k2, k2tog) twice, repeat from the * on each needle (7 sts per needle, 21 sts total remain)

Round 2: knit

Round 3: *k1, (k1, k2tog) twice, repeat from the * on each needle (5 sts per needle, 15 sts total remain)

Rounds 4 and 5: knit

Round 6: *k1, (k2tog) twice, repeat from the * on each needle (3 sts per needle, 9 sts total remain)

Rounds 7–9: knit

Round 10: (k1, k2tog) on each needle (2 sts per needle, 6 sts total remain)

Cut the yarn and thread the tail on a yarn needle. Pull through the remaining stitches, gather up tight to close the hole, and stitch to secure. Weave the end to the inside and trim.

Place the Rose Quartz hat on the head of the girl with the Rose Quartz dress. Let the hat roll naturally at the bottom edge and whipstitch to the head with a length of matching yarn threaded on a yarn needle. Weave end to the inside and trim.

pom-pom

With Slate, make a 1-inch pom-pom with 15 wraps. With the ends threaded on a yarn needle, whipstitch to the top point of the hat.

slate hat

With Slate, cast on 27 stitches, leaving a long tail and placing 9 stitches on each of three double-pointed needles. Join to work in the round, being careful not to twist the stitches. Place a stitch marker on the first stitch.

Knit every round until the hat measures 1 ¼ inches from the cast-on edge.

Decrease rounds
Round 1: *k1, (k2, k2tog) twice, repeat from the * on each needle (7 sts per needle, 21 sts total remain)
Round 2: knit
Round 3: *k1, (k1, k2tog) twice, repeat from the * on each needle (5 sts per needle, 15 sts total remain)
Round 4: knit
Round 5: *k1, (k2tog) twice, repeat from the * on each needle (3 sts per needle, 9 sts total remain)

Cut the yarn and thread the tail on a yarn needle. Pull through the remaining stitches, gather up tight to close the hole, and stitch to secure. Weave the end to the inside and trim.

Place the Slate hat on the head of the girl with the Slate dress. Let the hat roll naturally at the bottom edge, and whipstitch to the head with a length of matching yarn threaded on a yarn needle. Weave end to the inside and trim.

flower

TIP • If you choose not to crochet a flower, you can make a pom-pom with Rose Quartz to put on top of the hat.

With Rose Quartz and the crochet hook, chain 3 (see p. 11) and join with a slip stitch (see p. 12) to form a ring.
Next round: (chain 4, slip stitch into the ring), repeat 5 times.

Cut the yarn and pull through the stitch. Attach the flower to the top of the hat with the tail threaded on a yarn needle and a few stitches.

center of the flower
With Natural and two double-pointed needles used as straight needles, cast on 1 stitch loosely.
Row 1: kfb until there are 3 stitches on the right needle (3 sts)

Row 2: purl
Row 3: knit
Row 4: p3tog (1 st remains)

Cut the yarn and thread the tail on a yarn needle. Pull through the remaining stitch. Stitch loosely around the outside of the piece, gather up the stitches to make a ball, and stitch to secure. Attach the ball to the center of the flower with a few stitches. Weave the end to the inside and trim.

braids
Make Agate braids for the Slate hat sister:
Cut eighteen 7-inch lengths of Agate. Place 2 strands at a time on a yarn needle and pull through halfway on the side of the hat, 9 strands on each side. Braid the lengths. Tie with a length of Rose Quartz. Trim the ends.

Make Amber braids for the Rose Quartz hat sister:
Cut twelve 9-inch lengths of Amber. Place 2 strands at a time on a yarn needle and pull through halfway on the side of the hat, 6 strands on each side. Braid the lengths. Tie with a length of Rose Quartz. Trim the ends.

mouth and eyes
On each girl, embroider eyes with black embroidery floss and a yarn needle, using the photograph as a guide. Make 2 small straight stitches (see p. 14) for each eye. With red embroidery floss, take 2 small straight stitches to form a V shape. Weave the ends to the inside and trim.

arms (make 4)
With Natural, cast on 6 stitches, placing 2 stitches on each of three double-pointed needles. Join to work in the round, being careful not to twist the stitches. Place a stitch marker on the first stitch.

Knit every round until the arm measures 1 ½ inches from the cast-on edge.
Next round: (k1, m1, k1), repeat on each needle (3 sts per needle, 9 sts total)

Knit 3 rounds.

Cut the yarn and thread the tail on a yarn needle. Pull through the remaining stitches, gather up tight to close the hole, and stitch to secure. Weave to the inside and trim.

Stuff the hand with fiberfill. Tie a length of Natural around the wrist, securing with a half knot. Weave the ends to the inside and trim.

With the tail from the cast-on stitches threaded on a yarn needle, whipstitch the arms to the sides of the girls. Weave the ends to the inside and trim.

flower to hold

TIP • If you choose not to crochet a flower, you can make a knitted heart (see below) in Slate for the girl to hold.

Make a Slate flower with a Rose Quartz center the same as for the top of the hat. Attach the flower to the hands of the girl in the Rose Quartz dress with a few stitches so that the flower joins the hands in front of the body. Weave all ends to the inside and trim.

heart
With Rose Quartz and two double-pointed needles used as straight needles, cast on 2 stitches. Start at the top of the heart.
Row 1: kfb in each stitch (4 sts)
Row 2: purl
Cut the yarn and leave on the needle.

Make a second piece the same. On row 2, continue to purl across the first piece to join the two halves of the heart (8 sts).

Continue on to create the bottom of the heart:
Row 1: knit
Row 2: purl
Row 3: k1, ssk, k2, k2tog, k1 (6 sts remain)
Row 4: purl
Row 5: k1, ssk, k2tog, k1 (4 sts remain)
Row 6: purl
Row 7: ssk, k2tog, pass the first stitch over the second stitch and off the needle (1 st remains)

Cut the yarn and pull through the remaining stitch. Make a second heart. With a yarn needle and a tail, whipstitch the two heart pieces together, purl sides facing. Stuff the heart lightly with fiberfill before closing. Attach the heart to the hands of the girl with the Slate dress with a few stitches so the heart joins the hands in front of the body. Weave the ends to the inside and trim.

finishing
Turn both of the girls inside out. With the heads lined up and facing in opposite directions, and the wrong sides touching, take a few stitches with matching yarn and the yarn needle at the tops of the bodies. This will prevent the two girls from pulling apart. Turn the toy so the Rose Quartz girl is on the outside.

With Natural and the crochet hook, slip stitch through the purl (turning) rounds of both girls to join them at the bottom edge.

noncrochet alternative
With a length of Rose Quartz threaded on a yarn needle, whipstitch through the purl (turning) rounds of both girls to join them at the bottom edge. Weave all ends to the inside and trim.

egg to bluebird and a little nest, too

The beautiful simplicity and smoothness of eggs have always fascinated me, so much so that I had to include an egg in this reversible collection.

The small egg knits up in no time; the bird is just as easy, with only a few extra pieces to add on. However, I thought the egg looked kind of lonely sitting on a table by itself, so I knitted up a quick little double-seed-stitch nest with an optional picot edging. It's the necessary touch to make this set complete.

finished measurements

bluebird egg

- 3 inches tall, 3 inches long

nest

- 1¾ inches tall, 3½ inches wide

yarn

- O-Wool Balance (50% certified organic merino wool, 50% certified organic cotton; 130 yards/50 grams)
- Egg: 1 skein of Natural #1000
- Bluebird: 1 skein each in Opal #2026 and Amber #6122, and a small amount of Slate #2215 (for the eyes)
- Nest: 1 skein of Agate #8014

tools

- U.S. size 4 set of four double-pointed needles, or size needed to obtain gauge
- U.S. size F crochet hook (optional)
- Tape measure or ruler
- Yarn needle
- Scissors
- Stitch markers
- Polyester fiberfill, 1 small bag

gauge

- 6 stitches per inch in stockinette stitch

egg

With Natural, cast on 9 stitches, placing 3 stitches on each of three double-pointed needles. Join to work in the round, being careful not to twist the stitches. Place a stitch marker on the first stitch.

Round 1: knit

Round 2: (k1, m1, k1, m1, k1), repeat on each needle (5 sts per needle, 15 sts total)

Round 3: knit

Round 4: *k1, (m1, k1) four times, repeat from * on each needle (9 sts per needle, 27 sts total)

Round 5: knit

Round 6: (k1, m1, k8), repeat on each needle (10 sts per needle, 30 sts total)

Place a stitch marker on round 6 and leave it there. Turn and begin working back and forth in stockinette stitch (knit 1 row, purl 1 row). This will create the opening in the egg. Begin with a purl row. Work for 2 inches above the stitch marker. End with a knit row.

Begin working in the round again.

Decrease rounds

Round 1: (k3, k2tog), repeat to end of round (8 sts per needle, 24 sts total remain)

Round 2: knit

Round 3: (k2, k2tog), repeat to end of round (6 sts per needle, 18 sts total remain)

Round 4: knit

Round 5: (k1, k2tog), repeat to end of round (4 sts per needle, 12 sts total remain)

Round 6: knit

Round 7: k2tog, repeat to end of round (2 sts per needle, 6 sts total remain)

Cut the yarn and thread the tail on a yarn needle. Pull the end through the remaining stitches, gather up tight to close the hole, and stitch to secure. Thread the tail from the cast-on edge on a yarn needle, stitch through all of the cast-on stitches, and gather to close the hole. Stitch to secure. Weave all ends to the inside and trim.

bluebird

body

With Opal, complete the body the same as for the egg.

Place the egg inside the bluebird body, purl sides facing together. With a length of Natural threaded on a yarn needle, whipstitch around the opening of the egg and the body, aligning the edges. Weave the end to the inside and trim.

head

With Opal, cast on 9 stitches, placing 3 stitches on each of three double-pointed needles. Join to work in the round, being careful not to twist the stitches. Place a stitch marker on the first stitch.

Round 1: knit

Round 2: (k1, m1, k1, m1, k1), repeat on each needle (5 sts per needle, 15 sts total)

Round 3: knit

Round 4: (k1, m1, k3, m1, k1), repeat on each needle (7 sts per needle, 21 sts total)

Rounds 5–9: knit

Round 10: *(k1, k2tog), repeat to last stitch, k1, repeat from * on each needle (5 sts per needle, 15 sts total remain)

Thread the tail from the cast-on edge on a yarn needle. Stitch through all of the cast-on stitches, gather up tight to close the hole on the back of head, and stitch to secure. Leave the rest of the tail free to use later.

Stuff the head with fiberfill.

Round 11: knit

Round 12: (ssk, k1, k2tog), repeat on each needle (3 sts per needle, 9 sts total remain)

Round 13: knit

Finish stuffing.

Cut the yarn and thread the end on a yarn needle. Pull through the remaining stitches, gather up tight to close the hole, and stitch to secure. Weave the end to the inside and trim.

Thread the remaining tail from the cast-on edge on a yarn needle. Whipstitch the head to the top of the body, toward the front, using the photograph as a guide. Weave the end to the inside and trim.

wings (make 2)

With Opal and two double-pointed needles used as straight needles, cast on 3 stitches.

Row 1: k1, m1, k1, m1, k1 (5 sts)

Row 2: purl

Row 3: k1, m1, k3, m1, k1 (7 sts)

Row 4: purl

Rows 5–10: continue in stockinette stitch

Row 11: k1, ssk, k1, k2tog, k1 (5 sts remain)

Row 12: purl

Row 13: k1, ssk, k2tog (3 sts remain)

Row 14: purl

Row 15: slip 1, k2tog, pass the slipped stitch over the second stitch and off the needle (1 st remains)

Cut the yarn and thread on a yarn needle, then pull through the remaining stitch. Weave the bound-off end to the wrong side and trim. Thread the end from the cast-on edge on a yarn needle and whipstitch the wings to the top of the back of the body, using the photograph as a guide. Weave the ends to the inside and trim.

beak halves (make 2)

With Amber and two double-pointed needles used as straight needles, cast on 3 stitches.

Row 1: knit

Row 2: purl

Row 3: slip 1, k2tog, pass the slipped stitch over the second stitch and off the needle (1 st remains)

Cut the yarn and pull through the remaining stitch. With the ends threaded on a yarn needle, whipstitch the two beak pieces together, purl sides facing. Whipstitch the beak to the front of the head. Weave all ends to the inside and trim.

eyes

With a length of Slate threaded on a yarn needle, take a small straight stitch with 2 wraps (see p. 15) for each eye. Weave ends to the inside and trim.

nest

With Agate, cast on 60 stitches, placing 20 stitches on each of three double-pointed needles. Join to work in the round, being careful not to twist the stitches. Place a stitch marker on the first stitch.

Rounds 1 and 2: (k2, p2), repeat to end of round

Rounds 3 and 4: (p2, k2), repeat to end of round

Repeat rounds 1–4 until the nest measures 2 inches from the cast-on edge, ending with round 2 or 4.

Continue to knit every round.

Decrease rounds

Round 1: (k3, k2tog), repeat to end of round (16 sts per needle, 48 sts total remain)

Round 2: knit

Round 3: (k2, k2tog), repeat to end of round (12 sts per needle, 36 sts total remain)

Rounds 4 and 5: knit

Round 6: (k1, k2tog), repeat to end of round (8 sts per needle, 24 sts total remain)

Rounds 7 and 8: knit

Round 9: k2tog, repeat to end of round (4 sts per needle, 12 sts total remain)

Round 10: (k2, k2tog) on each needle (3 sts per needle, 9 sts total remain)

Cut the yarn and thread on a yarn needle. Pull the end through the remaining stitches, gather up tight to close the hole, and stitch to secure. Weave the end to the inside and trim.

picot edging (optional)

With Agate and the crochet hook, make a picot edge around the cast-on edge of the nest as follows:

chain 3, slip st in the same st, slip st in the next stitch, slip st in the next st repeat from * to * around the edge.

Cut the yarn and pull through the remaining stitch. Weave the end to the inside and trim.

sources

YARN

BLUE SKY ALPACAS, INC.
P.O. Box 88
Cedar, MN 55011
888-460-8862
www.blueskyalpacas.com

CASCADE YARNS
1224 Andover Park East
Tukwila, WA 98188
206-574-0440
www.cascadeyarns.com

DEBBIE BLISS YARNS
Distributed by Knitting Fever
P.O. Box 336
315 Bayview Avenue
Amityville, NY 11701
516-546-3600
www.knittingfever.com

DREAM IN COLOR YARN
www.dreamincoloryarn.com

KOIGU WOOL DESIGNS
P.O. Box 158
Chatsworth, Ontario N0H1G0
Canada
888-765-WOOL
www.koigu.com

MANOS DEL URUGUAY
Distributed by Design Source
P.O. Box 770
Medford, MA 02180
888-566-9970
www.manos.com.uy

O-WOOL
52 Seymour Street
Middlebury, VT 05753
802-388-1313
www.o-wool.com

NORO
Distributed by Knitting Fever
P.O. Box 336
315 Bayview Avenue
Amityville, NY 11701
516-546-3600
www.knittingfever.com

ROWAN YARNS AND NASHUA HANDKNITS
Distributed by Westminster Fibers
165 Ledge Street
Nashua, NH 03060
800-445-9276
www.knitrowan.com

SUNSHINE YARNS
www.sunshineyarns.com

YARNTINI SOCK YARN
Yarntini Etsy Shop at www.etsy
.com/shop.php?user_id=19334
or
www.yarntini.net

ZITRON TREKKING XXL
Distributed by Skacel Collection,
Inc.
800-255-1278
www.skacelknitting.com

BOUNCY BALLS

DCI PRODUCT
Décor Craft, Inc.
275 Westminster Street
Providence, RI 02903
877-947-1577
www.dcigift.com

WOOL ROVING AND FELT BALLS

ORNAMENTEA
509 N. West Street
Raleigh, NC 27603
919-834-6260
www.ornamentea.com

FABRIC

ANNA MARIA HORNER'S CHOCOLATE LOLLIPOP
www.annamariahorner.com

JO-ANN FABRIC AND CRAFT STORE
www.joann.com

for:
Wheels and axles
Polyester fiberfill
Poly pellets
Pipe cleaners
Embroidery floss
Foam padding

acknowledgments

Authors often work in solitude. However all books, in the end, are created by an enormous group effort. The group that created *Itty-Bitty Toys* is made up of incredible people who deserve my thanks.

Starting at the top, I extend my deepest gratitude to the talented Ann Bramson, my publisher, who has guided and encouraged me, gently pushing my knitting to a new level and in new directions.

Next up is my editor and sounding board, Trent Duffy. Not only is his guidance indispensable and his taste flawless, but he has a way of making me laugh that made putting this book together so much easier.

Also at Artisan, Jan Derevjanik provided a beautiful book design, and a cover that I just love. She brought the puzzle pieces together in a way no one else could.

Jaime Harder, my book publicist and friend, provided constant support, ideas, and cheerleading. Her talent and enthusiasm have brought me many wonderful opportunities that never would have come my way otherwise.

With her knitting and copy-editing expertise, Andrea Molitor made my words clear and shiny on the page.

I'd also like to acknowledge the invaluable assistance of the rest of the Artisan team: Amy Corley, Suzanne Lander, Nancy Murray, Quinn Rowan, Erin Sainz, and Barbara Peragine.

As she has on my two previous books, Liz Banfield brought my knitting projects alive through her magnificent photography. A huge dose of gratitude is due to the models of all ages and the parents of the little ones for participating in this book: Lilly, Ruby, Capri, Alisha, Nima, Quinn, Mario, Lily, Lauren, Cole, Anya, Roman, Lucca, Emma, Carrie, Grier, Charlotte, Michaelyn, Cooper, and Mason. Liz's assistant, Michelle DuPuis, helped to no end with this project and all of the Itty-Bitty books.

My family has been a constant source of support and inspiration throughout all of my knitting ventures, including this book. Without my loving husband and children, there would be no knitting. I owe my family immeasurable appreciation and gratitude.

Lastly, a huge thank-you goes out to the knitters who continue to read my blog, contact me, write comments, and send me photos of their babies, grandchildren, and completed projects. I am humbled to be included in their knitting lives.

k   knit

p   purl

k2tog   knit two stitches together as one stitch

p2tog   purl two stitches together as one stitch

ssk   slip two stitches one at a time as if to knit, knit these two stitches together through the back loops

kfb   knit into the front loop and then into the back loop of the same stitch

pfb   purl into the front loop and then into the back loop of the same stitch

m1   make one stitch by inserting the left needle from the front to the back under the bar in between the rightmost stitch on the left needle and the leftmost stitch on the right needle, making a loop on the left needle; knit the bar through the back loop

dpn(s)   double-pointed needle(s)

sl1   slip one stitch as if to purl

NOTES

ABOUT THE AUTHOR

Susan B. Anderson is the author of *Itty-Bitty Hats* and *Itty-Bitty Nursery*. Her knitting blog, susanbanderson.blogspot.com, gets more than 50,000 hits a month. Her popular series of ten knitting tutorials, appears on You Tube (www.youtube.com/SusanBAnderson). She lives in Madison, Wisconsin, with her husband and four children.